THE BLACK PRESIDENT

AND OTHER PLAYS

OTHER BOOKS BY JAMES SCHEVILL

The Stalingrad Elegies

Private Dooms and Public Destinations:
Poems 1945-1962

Sherwood Anderson: A Biography

The American Fantasies (poems)

The Right to Greet (poems)

High Sinners, Low Angels (musical play)

The Bloody Tenet (play)

Voices of Mass & Capital A (play for voices)

The Black
President

AND OTHER PLAYS

James Schevill

ALAN SWALLOW
DENVER

The
Bloody
Tenet

"...*liberavi animam meam: I have not
hid within my breast my soul's belief.*"
ROGER WILLIAMS *in his* The Bloody Tenet
of Persecution for Cause of Conscience

*To Marvin Halverson and the
National Council of Churches,
and to Lawrence Durgin and the
members of the Central Congregational
Church in Providence, Rhode Island,
where this play was first performed.*

CHARACTERS

IN THE PROLOGUE AND THE EPILOGUE:

THE EVANGELIST, *Mrs. Simpsen, a prominent American evangelist.*

THE JOURNALIST, *Edward Miller, a writer of books and articles on the history of religion.*

IN THE REMAINING SCENES:

GOVERNOR HAYNES, *Governor of Massachusetts Bay and Presiding Officer of the General Court.*

THOMAS DUDLEY, *Governor of the Bay before and after Haynes. At the time of Williams's trial, a leading magistrate.*

JOHN WINTHROP, *Ex-Governor of the Colony. Reduced to magistrate at the time of Williams's trial because of his "leniency to disaffected souls."*

JOHN COTTON, *Renowned theologian among the Puritans in England and the Calvinists on the continent. Who assured the world that the congregational system needed a vigorous magistracy. An implacable foe of Williams, Cotton dreamt of a theocracy modeled on the Biblical image of Israel.*

THOMAS HOOKER, *With Cotton a renowned minister, but a minister with a special reputation as a great preacher.*

ROGER WILLIAMS, *The defendant at the trial held in Hooker's Church, Newtown, October 8, 1635.*

MARY WILLIAMS, *His wife.*

CANONICUS, *The Chief of the Narragansett Indians.*

SIR EDWARD COKE, *Chief Justice of the Star Chamber under Queen Elizabeth. The great English lawyer and mentor of Williams.*

Note: Since Canonicus does not speak, this part can be doubled. The cast for performance, then, consists of eight men and two women.

8

PROLOGUE

SCENE I: The church is dark. Through the darkness the choir is
heard singing "Wondrous Love."

> What wondrous love is this,
> Oh my soul, oh my soul,
> What wondrous love is this,
> Oh my soul.
>
> What wondrous love is this
> That caused the Lord of bliss
> To bear the dreadful curse
> For my soul, for my soul,
> To bear the dreadful curse
> For my soul.
>
> When I was sinking down,
> Sinking down, sinking down,
> When I was sinking down,
> Sinking down.
>
> When I was sinking down
> Beneath God's righteous frown
> Christ laid aside His crown
> For my soul, for my soul,
> Christ laid aside His crown
> For my soul.
>
> And when from death I'm free
> I'll sing on, I'll sing on,
> And when from death I'm free
> I'll sing on.
>
> And when from death I'm free
> I'll sing and joyful be
> And through eternity
> I'll sing on, I'll sing on,
> And through eternity
> I'll sing on.

The light comes up to reveal the JOURNALIST waiting for the
EVANGELIST. A banner, reading THE TEMPLE OF RADIANT

9

REDEMPTION, hangs on the wall. The JOURNALIST is a middle-aged intellectual, shrewd, aggressive and cynical. Nervously, he looks around the Temple before he speaks.

JOURNALIST:
> She's late ... I'll bet she keeps everyone waiting ... All these statues
> ... *(He gestures with disgust around the Temple.)* I thought Prot-
> estants had gotten rid of idols.
> But she seems to have added a few of her own ...
> *(He looks at the banner.)*
> The Gospel of Radiant Redemption . . . There's a
> Simple-minded American evangelist for you.
> The latest tricks of Public Relations ... *(Then bitterly):*
> I used to think of myself as a religious historian.
> Now I'm just a reporter who runs after evangelists
> For interviews ... Sh ... here she comes ...
>> *He is startled as the* EVANGELIST *makes an impressive entrance.*
>> *She is dressed in a dazzling, long white gown, with a red sash*
>> *across the front. There is no doubt of the magnetism of her per-*
>> *sonality.*

EVANGELIST *(extending her hand regally):*
> Mr. Miller? I'm sorry to keep you waiting.

JOURNALIST:
> Thank you for seeing me, Mrs. Simpsen. *(Then ironically):*
> Don't worry about keeping me waiting.
> A journalist only kills time.

EVANGELIST:
> Is this your first visit to
> My Temple of Radiant Redemption?

JOURNALIST:
> Yes, I'm afraid it is ...

EVANGELIST:
> Then stop a moment and listen ... *(She stops him imperiously.)*
> Listen to the spirit of our ancestors
> Who sing the Gospel of Radiant Redemption.

JOURNALIST *(puzzled):*
  The ancestors of your Gospel?

EVANGELIST *(sweeping her arm around the church):*
  There they are, in the air of eternity.
  Sweet in the sunlight of His grace,
  The heroes who have bled for Jesus.
  Do you hear that voice in the corner?

JOURNALIST:
  I don't hear anything.

EVANGELIST:
  That is the soul of Saint Peter, crucified downwards,
  Who knew the secret irony of a crucifixion
  Forces the traitors still to look up at you.
  (She is about to lead him to another corner, but he stops her.)

JOURNALIST:
  But Saint Peter was a Catholic martyr...

EVANGELIST *(brushing this off firmly):*
  Religious heroes, Mr. Miller, belong to Jesus
  And not to any one religious order. *(She points to another corner.)*
  In this blessed corner of my Temple
  Prays the martyr, John Huss, as the cruel flames
  Burnt the flesh of earth from his body.
  Jesus has always demanded sacrifice
  To escape the hot temptation of Hell.

JOURNALIST:
  Perhaps there is a danger of conformity in religion
  And heretics are created as scapegoats, but
  The saints and martyrs of God need no earthly recognition.
  Why do you make them into a personal gallery of heroes?

EVANGELIST:
  We forget their sacrifices too easily.
  Religion has need of heroes today.

JOURNALIST:
  You don't understand what I mean.
  By praising martyrs and heretics

11

As heroes of religious revolt,
Aren't you destroying the unity
Of organized churches and setting up
New symbols of separation . . . ?

EVANGELIST:

There's nothing wrong with symbols.
I don't think God is a realistic geographer
Of Heaven and Hell, Mr. Miller.
Each soul is a fire escape and a fire trap
At the same time, you must know that.

JOURNALIST *(pointedly)*:

The danger of religious rebels is that
They interpret scripture for their own ends.
That's why the early Christian fathers
Moved back from the cloudy symbols of the word
To the traditions of the acts of Jesus.

EVANGELIST:

Religion has no meaning
Unless the symbol and the act are one.
Don't try to deceive me, Mr. Miller.
The danger of the scholar is that
He wastes all his time poring over words
And finally divides the act and the symbol
Into two false worlds.

JOURNALIST *(nettled)*:

Perhaps your're right. That may be the scholar's danger,
But what is the danger of the evangelist
Who creates a world of romantic isolation
Split apart from all other Christian churches?

EVANGELIST:

I don't split myself away from other churches.
Wherever I preach throughout the country,
I try to cooperate with all churches
On the March for Christ through an extensive follow-up system.

JOURNALIST:
   Isn't there a risk of turning religion into Public Relations
   With your March for Christ and your follow-up systems?

EVANGELIST *(scornfully)*:
   Religion is not a guest home for Sunday visits
   As you conformist intellectuals would make it.
   You've lost your spirit working for a magazine
   That treats religion like a mummy in a museum.
   Come to the services in my Temple, Mr. Miller,
   And throw away your crutches of cynicism!

JOURNALIST *(Stiffly)*:
   I think religion is a private matter between man and God.
   Preaching to crowds in a Temple or on a street corner may
   Hypnotize them, but it doesn't bring them closer to God.
   This idea of mass religion is why
   We've never had a real American heretic.

EVANGLELIST:
   A street corner for the soul is as good as a study
   If the brain will descend to the smell of the street.
   And you're wrong about an American martyr. There has been one.
   You've even written about him. This is his heroic corner
   In my Temple of Radiant Redemption. *(She points)*

JOURNALIST:
   Who do you mean?

EVANGELIST *(fervently)*:
   Roger Williams, the founder of religious freedom,
   The gentle soul who separated the church
   Once and for all from the tyranny of state control.

JOURNALIST *(protesting)*:
   That's what I mean about your gallery of heroes.
   You're not talking about the real Williams,
   But a fantasy of your own creation.
   Williams was hardly a gentle soul
   And he certainly wasn't a martyr.
   His opponents, Governor Haynes, Thomas Dudley,

13

John Winthrop, and the great ministers,
Thomas Hooker and John Cotton—
They were deeply religious men.

EVANGELIST:
Many false religious fires
Shine from the walls of Hell.

JOURNALIST:
I'm surprised to hear *you* say that.
The Puritans weren't insincere about Williams.
They thought he was a kind of stubborn crank.

EVANGELIST:
Sometimes God loves the stubborn shepherd
More than the meek sheep, Mr. Miller.

JOURNALIST:
What do you really know about Williams?
Do you remember his interpretation of the parable in Matthew 13?

EVANGELIST:
You mean the parable when God commands men to let alone
The weeds to grow up with the wheat until the harvest.

JOURNALIST:
Yes. Williams said the church lives wildly
In the wilderness of the world, and
Cannot ever find absolute truth. The weeds
In the parable, to Williams, were false Christians ...

EVANGELIST *(emphatically)*:
Mr. Miller, there are false *everythings* today.

JOURNALIST *(pointedly)*:
Williams called these false Christians
Strange professors of the name of Jesus,
Sowers of ignorance and error in the night ...

EVANGELIST *(indignantly)*:
You imply that he would call me a strange professor of Jesus?

JOURNALIST *(shrugging)*:
I'm only a journalist. I'm asking you

If your Temple of Radiant Redemption
Is another one of the isolated groups
That grow wildly in our country today?

EVANGELIST *(calmly and with great confidence)*:
Religion, I think, is not a bed of roses.
Your Williams chained in the false light of history
Is not as real as my view of his message of spiritual freedom.
You have no right to judge the heroes inside the Lord's garden.

JOURNALIST:
I don't judge anything. This is your Temple.

EVANGELIST:
The Lord knows I prefer the quiet of a chapel,
But the radiation of His eternal will
Drives my spirit to help men toward His grace.

JOURNALIST:
Is that why you play the role of Christ
When you stage the crucifixion every year?
Isn't that a heresy of pride
That cuts away the grace of God?

EVANGELIST:
No one can proclaim himself a heretic.
Only the Lord has that sacred power:
If there was no one to challenge conformity
The prosecutors of heresy would survive
In their cold masks of security.

JOURNALIST:
Without prosecution, there would be no society of law.

EVANGELIST:
No prosecutor can represent the love of God.
How can you know the torment of a Roger Williams
When he stands alone against a power of men?

JOURNALIST:
I don't know and I admit it, but I know
What Williams has come to mean in history.
You aren't the only one to distort his life.

15

In Geneva his statue stands as one of the leaders
Of the Protestant Revolution, the hero
Who separated the church from the state.
His knotty mind has been simplified to this one point,
And from that point flower all of the weird sects—
The strange professors of Jesus—
Who grow wildly in our country today.

EVANGELIST:
The strange professor of Jesus may be a danger
But God did not create every man to be ordinary.
It would cost the loss of many souls
If I turned from the Lord's power of radiant redemption.
I have often thought about the trial of Roger Williams
And I am sure there was only one central issue,
The true love of God . . .

JOURNALIST *(protesting)*:
But the trial of Williams was a complicated one. There were many
issues involved . . .

EVANGELIST *(ignoring this)*:
God has willed us to remember only the simple issue
Of freedom to love God in our own way.

JOURNALIST *(angrily)*:
How could Williams, with his complicated mind,
Ever think of simplifying God?

EVANGELIST *(triumphantly)*:
Didn't he teach the savage Indians?
In the same way Christ taught an almost illiterate people
And today we must call back that simplicity
And teach the power of God's love and fire!
*(She is close to him, scorning him with the fire of her voice as the
scene blacks out and the choir is heard singing)*:

The land is fair, the air is soft,
The Good Lord guides our hand
And all that stirs has a final word
To say that He dwells away, afar, alone.

16

His eye is bright, His justice swift,
He smiles all sinners down;
And every sin that glows like coal
Reveals that He dwells away, afar, alone.

The sea is deep with sunken ships,
Each wave brings death to a wife;
The whitecapped waves and the soaring gulls
Reveal that He dwells away, afar, alone.

Praise to His name, our Lord, our God,
His name brings fire to the lip.
The glowing soil at the sinner's knee
Reveals that He dwells away, afar, alone.

SCENE II: *Hooker's Church. Newtown, now Cambridge, Massachusetts, 1635.*

HOOKER *(enters with* COTTON, DUDLEY, WINTHROP *and* HAYNES*):*
It is a humble church, Governor Haynes. We have no comforts here.

HAYNES:
But a strong fortress for God's spirit, Mr. Hooker.
Every man in Massachusetts Bay honors your preaching
And I am told your voice haunts all the pulpits in the colony.

HOOKER:
If I am honored with a voice, Sir,
It is to speak God's word in this new state.

WINTHROP *(to* HAYNES*):*
Why did you ask us here?

HAYNES:
It is the case of Roger Williams of which an end must be made.

WINTHROP:
I cannot judge this case
For I have been his friend
Despite his nature of dissent.

17

HAYNES:

You were honored, Mr. Winthrop,
As first governor of all this Bay . . .

DUDLEY:

But then reduced to magistrate
For leniency to disaffected souls . . .

HAYNES:

Please, Mr. Dudley. *(then, to* WINTHROP*)*
This a case, Sir, in which we must request your aid
For we know your love of God and value all your judgments.

WINTHROP:

Mr. Williams is a man well-liked
Though his views seem wild and crankish.

DUDLEY:

Especially well-liked in old England.

HAYNES:

That is where our problem rests.
Mr. Williams demands the right of complete separation
For any church within this colony.
He demands this rigorous separation
Not only from the English church, which we might tolerate,
But also from our theocratic Bay authority.
He has many influential English friends
Who listen when he writes against our magistrates.

WINTHROP:

Has he taken action to support these views?

HAYNES:

In order to foster this separation
He has sent letters to all our churches in the Bay
Accusing our magistrates of tyrannical interference
With the free powers of his Salem congregation.

DUDLEY:

This is a rage of rebellion, Sir. You cannot deny that.

WINTHROP:

It is a wrong, but more I think
A case of temper than ill will and plotting.

DUDLEY:

Plotting or temper makes no difference
To the welfare of the state. Both must be punished.
We cannot let this rebel split apart
Our unity of magistrates and ministers.

WINTHROP:

What is it you mean to do, Mr. Dudley?

DUDLEY:

Mr. Williams must be tried before the General Court.

WINTHROP:

I ask to be excused.

HAYNES:

You must assist us else the colony is split.
The danger we face is absolute and clear.
We are only a small settlement
Surrounded by savage and heathen enemies.
If we lose our central authority
Our state cannot long survive.

DUDLEY *(to* WINTHROP*)*:

Would you have our land dissolve
And all your reputation gone
Because a man of overweening pride
Thrusts down our Bay his knife of separation?

WINTHROP:

He never seemed to my friendship
A man possessed by devil's pride. *(Turning to* HOOKER *and* COTTON
for support)
Has he been argued with by our honored ministers?

HAYNES:

I asked Mr. Cotton to contest with him
Because I thought no one could deny
The sacred scholarship of our leading theologian.

HOOKER *(to* WINTHROP*):*
  Mr. Cotton has just returned from long and bitter days
  In Salem and will tell you of his futile argument.

COTTON:
  Sirs, I do not seek your praise of scholarship.
  This is an unpleasant task where the word of the Lord
  Is conflicted with in practice.
  When I visited Mr. Williams I found him sick in bed
  Where he did read with feverish haste
  To find support within the Bible.

DUDLEY:
  He cannot find a heresy in every town
  Within the sacred fury of the Bible.

WINTHROP:
  Is it a serious illness?

COTTON:
  Mainly a sickness of the mind I think
  That failed to keep his words from running riot.

WINTHROP:
  You do not judge him by his independent tongue?

COTTON:
  I have no doubt of his sincerity,
  But he has a head that runs around
  And begs all constant reason
  With its shifting roundabout.
  He is a lion for separation, so strong for it,
  There seems nothing left but God from which to separate;
  And when I did strap him down on separation
  He wriggled out on oaths of loyalty,
  And when I questioned him on loyalty
  He shifted to attack the magistrates
  For threatening his Salem church.

HAYNES:
  It is a grave accusation that threatens all our government.

WINTHROP:

    Let us not forget we are fled from an England
    Where the laws of men warped the peaceful ways of God
    Into a force that shattered peace.
    We must beware of civil law.

COTTON:

    That was his question of me, asking, in Christ's words,
    Should we not render unto Caesar the things that are Caesar's,
    And unto God the things that are God's?
    But in our New England we have no forcing hand of Caesar;
    We have no civil government but stems from God's holy word.
    I asked Mr. Williams, would he have a Caesar here in the Lord's
        state?
    And he answered, there is only one Lord's state,
    The Bible's Israel, and it was doomed by God.
    He is a man who reads his Bible like a dreamer
    And cannot see the factual hand of the Lord.

WINTHROP:

    We must take care in judging dreamers.
    A state that sharpens laws to pointed spears
    Tears all dissent and dream on cruel steel
    And sinks into oblivion like a stain of blood.
    Was it not Joseph's brethren who said scornfully,
    "Behold, this dreamer cometh"?

HAYNES:

    Sir, I think no one takes this trial lightly.
    If Mr. Williams is a dreamer, it is the act of his dream
    We will judge and not the fantasy of his vision. *(To* COTTON*)*
    What did he say to his letters attacking our magistrates?

COTTON:

    He justified them as the freedom of his conscience.
    Conscience moves in his every word like a devious worm
    In underground soil until no man knows its way or goal.

WINTHROP:

    Is is not true then, Mr. Cotton,
    If we fail to uphold the freedom of conscience
    We make a mockery of our new state?

COTTON:

It is a sacred duty, Mr. Winthrop,
Yet what is conscience but the soul of every man?
And while we must not punish the freedom of this soul before God,
We must punish any soul if it sins against itself,
For the Lord commanded Moses, "Thou shalt have no other God
    before me."
How then can a soul find salvation if it be permitted
To worship false idols under the disguise of conscience-freedom?

HAYNES:

What did Mr. Williams answer to this thought?

COTTON:

He did evade it by answering, the Lord also commanded
"Thou shalt not bear false witness against thy neighbor."
But who has cried false witness against his neighbor?
I tell you it is a head that runs around.

DUDLEY:

But though confused a danger to our unity.
He must be stopped from sins against his conscience.

WINTHROP:

And we, Sir, must be careful of sins to ours. *(To* COTTON)
Did you question him further on the magistrates
In addition to the Salem incident?

COTTON:

He has a general principle, a storm of clouds in his words,
That magistrates may not punish any breach of the First Table of
    the Decalogue.

HAYNES:

If this should ever occur our civil officers
Could not even enforce the Sabbath.

COTTON:

Then I quoted him the declaration of the First Helvetic Conference
    that:
"The chief office of the magistrate is to defend religion
And to take care that the word of God is purely preached."

WINTHROP:

　He did deny that?

COTTON:

　No, but he stressed the words *defend* and *take care*
　And called them words of peace and not attack,
　And hinted darkly of invented devotions to the God of heaven.

HAYNES:

　What meant he by "invented devotions"?

COTTON:

　It is hard to find the force of clarity
　On the surface of a muddy stream,
　But it seemed he meant the magistrates.
　He thinks it wrong that clergymen have vested interests
　Together with the magistrates upon our state.
　But what these vested interests are,
　And where the ministers that sin, he cannot say.

HAYNES:

　What do you think of this, Mr. Hooker?

HOOKER:

　I have known Mr. Williams and liked him,
　But he is a danger wrapped in the cloak of simplicity.
　It is the seeming innocents who carry
　Tight beneath their friendly love the flame of a despotic will
　That burns the union of the church and state.

HAYNES *(To* WINTHROP*):*

　Are you convinced, Mr. Winthrop,
　Of the need for this reluctant trial?

WINTHROP:

　Must it be a session of the General Court?
　With time, can we not persuade him
　By a delegation of more ministers?

COTTON:

　It is too late for that, but there is merit in your thought.
　What if besides the magistrates and deputies upon the General Court,
　We summon our ministers within the Bay?

Such a trial, with all our eminence of leadership,
Held here in this honored church of Mr. Hooker,
Must persuade him of his errors
And bring his soul back to aid our colony.

WINTHROP:
When would you hold the trial?

DUDLEY:
It must be soon for many churches threaten separation.

HAYNES:
Let us set the morning of October 8.

WINTHROP:
But he is sick upon his bed.
It is just to force him to attend so soon?

DUDLEY:
Mr. Cotton thinks it but a sickness of the mind.

COTTON:
It seemed a sickness that can stand a trial's debate,
And sometimes in a mind's dark fever,
The light of grace strikes suddenly.

HAYNES:
Our magistrates and deputies must be notified.

DUDLEY:
I will arrange for them.

HAYNES *(To* COTTON *and* HOOKER*)*:
And you, Sirs, I ask you to approach our ministers.

HOOKER:
We will do so.

HAYNES *(To* WINTHROP*)*:
You will attend, Mr. Winthrop, and lend us your aid?

WINTHROP *(hesitating)*:
I will hear the evidence.
   As the scene ends, the choir is heard singing

24

"DAVID'S LAMENTATION" *by* WILLIAM BILLINGS:

> *"David the King was grieved and moved,*
> *He went to his chamber, his chamber and wept.*
> *And as he wept, he wept and said:*
> *'O my son, O my son,*
> *Would to God I had died,*
> *Would to God I had died.'"*

SCENE III: *The home of* ROGER WILLIAMS. *Only a rough cot is needed to indicate the change of setting.*

WILLIAMS *(enters, tired and dusty):*
  Mary! I am home. *(He slumps down on the edge of the cot.)*

MARY *(enters):*
  You were gone so long I was worried. Are you ill again?

WILLIAMS:
  No, only tired and weak. Give me some water.
  I have been riding many hours.

MARY *(She gives him some water and feels his forehead.)*
  You are feverish. Why did you ride?

WILLIAMS:
  I had to ride today. And would not ride against your wishes.
  If you had known you would have begged me stay at home.

MARY:
  You were not busy with your trading duties?

WILLIAMS:
  No, I rode this morning to keep a secret meeting with Canonicus.

MARY:
  Canonicus?

WILLIAMS:
  Yes, the chief of the Narrangansett Indians.

25

MARY:

But our people all distrust him.
They fear him for planning
Savage crimes against our settlers.

WILLIAMS:

The summons I expected came yesterday.
I must stand trial in three days
Before the General Court in Newtown.

MARY:

The General Court!

WILLIAMS:

They have charged me with heresy
And called me a danger to the state.
They have even asked their ministers to attend
And placed the trial in Hooker's Church
To sharpen my guilt under God's law.

MARY:

Why then did Mr. Cotton visit you?
You were companions in the flight from England.

WILLIAMS:

He sought to persuade me of my errors, but failed.
Mary, I know they will be strict at this General Court...

MARY:

They cannot take your life?

WILLIAMS:

Some might have the wish, but I do not think
They dare so far although I have bitter enemies.

MARY:

What will happen to you?

WILLIAMS:

I think they will plot to send me back to England,
Convicted of disloyalty, in a winter passage of shame
Before my friends. But I will not go.

26

MARY:

They are many and hold the power.

WILLIAMS:

I have bought land in Narragansett
From their chief, Canonicus,
And mean to found a colony there if I am exiled.

MARY:

Another colony? How can you trust this heathen savage?

WILLIAMS:

Mary, we have been guilty of great wrong to the Indians.
We have seized their land by force,
But I have made peace with Canonicus.

MARY:

What peace is there in another colony?
I remember Mr. Cotton preaching once from *Samuel:*
Moreover, I will appoint a place for my people Israel,
And I will plant them that they may dwell
In a place of their own and move no more.
They are words I have never forgotten.

WILLIAMS:

Would you have me compromise
And tell the Court all my acts were lies?

MARY:

How can I judge you? I am your wife.
Oh, I would help you but I have nothing of your learning.
I will always follow you and do as you ask me,
But do not ask my understanding.

WILLIAMS:

Do you think I understand myself?
What dreamer understands the wilderness of his dream?
Riding by the ocean this dawn
Where the boats rocked at their anchors,
I saw the sentinel gulls perched on their high posts
In patient time, and the leaves drifted deathwards
Back to matter on the still water, and I thought,

27

It is always God's time in the sun.
He moves towards birth and death in His mysterious moment
And no man stands the luxury of His light.
How then can I understand the shadows of my dream?
But I think if that dream ever were extinguished
My little source of God's light is gone.

MARY:

Although I cannot share your dream
I would not fight against it.

WILLIAMS:

We have a child, Mary, and you expect
Another one within two months.
No one will harm you here. They would not dare that,
And when I have a free settlement in the land
I shall, with God's love, call by the name of Providence,
I will send for you and the children.
Is it selfish of me to hold my views?

MARY:

You were never a selfish man. Last month,
When you separated from our Salem church as teacher,
You let me go on praying there
Despite the whisperings of many tongues.

WILLIAMS:

It is your own conscience, Mary,
And I have no right to interfere with that.

MARY:

You always speak of conscience as mine or yours.
Has not our family a conscience too?

WILLIAMS:

Mary!

MARY:

I cannot help my tongue.
When we fled by ship from England
Our company was Christian men.
Now you deal with heathen Indians.

WILLIAMS:

Your words are unjust. Here in the Bay
The Indian is our torment and we persecute him
With a bloody tenet because his religion is not ours.
But I have bought this soil from Canonicus.
His tribe will not disturb our settlement.

MARY:

And what will happen to our children? It is a risk for them.

WILLIAMS:

The children will be safe. I will not send for you
Until I prove my faith with the Indians.

MARY:

I pray that your pride of conscience
Does not forsake the word of God.

WILLIAMS:

You must not judge me, Mary.
Conscience is only a persuasion
Fixed in the mind and heart of man
That forces him to choose his way to God.
I have seen the Gates of Hell and through them
Enter preachers as well as lawyers, artisans, farmers,
Men who had no conscience in their choice.

MARY:

Why must your conscience lead to my bitter isolation?
Why must I endure this loneliness?
An exile from my husband, and then another exile
In the wilderness from our holy church. *(She is crying and fighting to control herself.)*

WILLIAMS:

This will not be an exile, Mary.
Do you remember what the Lord said to Rebekah?
"Two nations are in thy womb, and the one people
Shall be stronger than the other people
And the elder shall serve the younger."
Here in the Bay I think we are the elder nation

And have failed to find the true peace of God's will,
But there in Narragansett we of the Bay
Shall found and serve the younger nation,
That men may live and worship in peace
And the land be open before us. *(He pauses.)*
Mary, if all this is my vanity
Tell me and I will act against it.

MARY *(controlling herself):*

I think no woman can judge a man's pride
Before the Lord, least of all a wife her husband.
It is my duty to go with you where you will go.

WILLIAMS:

I would not have it a mere duty.

MARY *(after a slight pause):*
You must rest. I will get you food. *(She goes out.)*

WILLIAMS *(he picks up the Bible and begins to read):*
"And Isaac intreated the Lord for his wife, because she was barren:
and the Lord was intreated of him, and Rebekah his wife conceived.
And the children struggled together within her; and she said, 'If it
be so, why am I thus?' And she went to enquire of the Lord. And
the Lord said unto her, 'Two nations are in thy womb . . .' "
*Worn out, he falls asleep. The choir is heard singing very softly,
"*DAVID THE KING.*" The lights dim suddenly and the bloody,
shadowy outline of the Indian chief,* CANONICUS, *is seen.* WILLIAMS
starts up.

WILLIAMS:

Canonicus! Fever burns my brain.
This is a vision of blood. What have we done in New England?
Under the cross of the living God, with a prayer of Thanksgiving,
We have possessed the dead stones from the Indians,
With a greed for great portions of land
And a depraved appetite for the vanity of power.
Oh, Canonicus, can I ever make peace with you?
In the bloody thoughts you bring me
What are all the wars of this world about
But for greater dishes and bowls of gain?

30

We will drive your people from your land
And burn your crude huts and kill your warriors
And you will murder our Christian settlers.
But if you will let me build my Providence
Perhaps a small memory of gentle peace
Between the Indian and white man will live on,
A grain of conscience for the lies of vanity.
Having bought truth dear we must not sell it cheap,
Not the least grain of it for the whole world,
Least of all for the bitter sweetening
Of a little vanishing pleasure, for a little
Puff of reputation from the changeable breath of men,
For the broken bags of riches that fall from eagles' wings,
For a dream of those which on our deathbed
Vanish and leave tormenting flames behind them.
What are the leaves and flowers and smoke of earthly things
About which we poor fools disquiet ourselves in vain?
Eternity, eternity, is our business.

The figure of CANONICUS *disappears. Agitated,* WILLIAMS *begins to read from the Bible again.*

"And he dreamed, and, behold, a ladder set up on the earth, and the top of it reached to heaven: and, behold, the angels of the Lord ascending and descending on it. And, behold, the Lord stood above it, and said, 'I am the Lord God of Abraham thy father, and the God of Isaac: the land whereon thou liest, to thee will I give it, and to thy seed; and thy seed shall be as the dust of the earth, and thou shalt spread abroad to the west, and to the east, and to the north, and to the south ...' "

The figure of SIR EDWARD COKE *appears. He is richly clothed in Elizabethan formal dress in contrast to the severe Puritan clothing of* WILLIAMS.

COKE:
Sir, you speak too soon of eternity ...

WILLIAMS:
Who are you?

COKE:
The dust of the earth of which you read.

31

WILLIAMS:

Sir Edward Coke!

COKE:

I thought your conscience had shadowed out a thought of me.

WILLIAMS:

I have never forgotten you.

COKE:

You remember my power then?

WILLIAMS:

I could never forget the Chief Justice of England.

COKE:

After the death of Queen Elizabeth,
When I continued as Chief Justice
Of the Star Chamber under King James,
I made you my chief stenographer.

WILLIAMS:

Yes . . . there in the Star Chamber, which I came to think of
As a web of spiders weaving testimony of the
King's intrigues, I learned to dream of God.

COKE:

Was it of God you dreamt, or of the noblemen
Whose deaths I caused, beheaded Essex and Southampton?

WILLIAMS:

I felt their shadows in that courtroom always—
Trials in which I knew you took the throne's part,
But knew not your exact role.

COKE:

You knew the role I played, but shut your eyes
For conscience-ease. You were a man who wrote shorthand
As well as any clerk in England and enjoyed
The pleasure of your trust, the glitter of
London's dancing fairs, the full-dress executions on Tower Hill.

WILLIAMS:

Do not mock me! I was born into the Age of Puritans
And never knew the rule of Queen Elizabeth.

32

COKE:
True, she died the year that you were born,
But under King James's rule, you saw me preside
Over the trial of the poisoners of Sir Thomas Overbury.

WILLIAMS:
I hated all the nobles' cheating pomp and scorn of God!

COKE:
You hated me when the wardrobe mistress, Mrs. Turner,
A conspirator in the Overbury poisoning,
The inventor of a yellow starch for cuffs, took the stand
And I called her, "Whore, bawd, papist!" And had her hanged.
You remember the executioner wore yellow starched cuffs.

WILLIAMS:
I did hate the rule of James which brought a
Bloody autumn of persecution for cause of conscience.

COKE:
What a peacock your conscience is
Preening itself with illusion.
Despite your revulsion from the Star Chamber
You sucked willingly on my power,
Attended college on my recommending word,
Nourished yourself on my patronage.

WILLIAMS:
I did ever admire your belief in the Common Law
And your fight for parliamentary rights against the King
Until I came to know the truer law of God's will.

COKE:
Hypocrite! You became a puritan as a boy,
A step your tailor father hated and so you hated your parents too!

WILLIAMS:
The tailor and the cruel court were bound together.
Without the tailor who could be a fop
And preen and ape indecent ways?

33

COKE:

This is your curse of conscience then, to hate your parents,
And all your youth to act the pure and godly rebel
While serving me inside the Star Chamber.

WILLIAMS *(agonizingly)*:

I did ever dream of God, even in the Star Chamber!

COKE:

Even when you became a minister and chaplain
In the household of Sir William Masham at Otes
And fell in love with Lady Masham's daughter, Jug?
This lust was your dream of God?

WILLIAMS:

It is not true!

COKE:

But Lady Masham would not have you
As a low-born husband for her daughter
And so your conscience sank again.
In springtime of your sex and bitterness
You married your wife, Mary—
Who was nothing but Jug's maid.

WILLIAMS:

Devil, devil! Why do you torture me
When I did always love you?

COKE:

Devil of conscience perhaps,
Curse of pride. Is it not true?

WILLIAMS:

No, it is ... half true. My pride caused me bitter words
Against the Lady Masham, and my need turned me to her maid,
My wife, Mary, whom I learned to love.

COKE:

But married from lust.

WILLIAMS:

Married from need of love perhaps, but not from lust.

34

It is true I feared God for my hate against Lady Masham
Who thought me low-born for her daughter;
This was my sin of pride.

COKE (*scornfully*):
What is the reward you seek then?

WILLIAMS:
I live only for the fear and grace of God.

COKE:
How can you hope for the grace of God
When you say you live in fear of His name?
Did not John preach: "Perfect love casts out fear"?

WILLIAMS:
You are the tempter conscience dreads,
And yet I think no human love is perfect.
The true love of God never casts out
The true fear of God, but only that which is
False and counterfeit, the fear of beasts and slaves.
Men must learn to live with fear before they come to love
And so it was the spirit of the fear of God
Poured down upon the Lord Jesus himself.

COKE:
Go to your trial of man's law then,
Go with your fear and seek your hope;
Go with your lust and seek deliverance;
Go with your pride and seek humility;
But remember your English past in the Star Chamber,
The parents whom you hated, and the passion of your springtime love.
He vanishes.

WILLIAMS:
Mary! Mary!

MARY (*enters*):
Did you call? Is it pain again?

WILLIAMS:
Pain of conscience, Mary.

I dreamt I saw Sir Edward Coke
Who called me back to the Star Chamber.

MARY:

You must not go to court so soon.
It is cruel in your sickness to make you attend.

WILLIAMS:

I must go if God wills it.

MARY:

How can you judge God's will?
Can you not convince them of your innocence?

WILLIAMS:

Mary, I cannot convince even you
That I do not act from pride only.

MARY:

A proud man is like a tower in the sun.
Who can tell if the tower points to God
Or the vanity of man's dream?
You are my husband. I cannot judge your pride.

WILLIAMS:

Mary, I have done you wrong. I would not lose your love.

MARY:

Love is not the daring of a dream
But of a daily harmony. When men and women marry
I think they know little of love
Which comes only with living together.

WILLIAMS:

We have been married six years, Mary.
Can you love my stubborn soul?

MARY:

I pray against your pride
And do not understand your actions
But I know you seek in them the grace of God.
I have not your words, but you have my love.

WILLIAMS:

Mary, I am sick in mind. From my pride
Humility can only flow with your love.
He turns away from her, deeply moved.
I must study now. *(He picks up the Bible.)*

MARY *(going to him):*

You must rest, not study.

WILLIAMS:

I cannot rest until God's will is done at this trial.
The Father of Spirits is my witness of the search
My spirit has made after Him in all passages from the Bible.
The fruits I have suffered and gained from this sickness
I hope I shall never forget. Mary, let me read to you.
*She sits beside him on the cot and he begins to read to her from the
Bible, from the Twenty-Fourth Psalm:*

*The earth is the Lord's, and the fulness thereof;
The world, and they that dwell therein.
For he hath founded it upon the seas,
And established it upon the floods.*

*Who shall ascend into the hill of the Lord?
He that hath clean hands and a pure heart;
Or who shall stand in His holy place?
Who hath not lifted up his soul into vanity, nor sworn deceitfully.*

*He shall receive the blessing from the Lord,
And righteousness from the God of his salvation.
This is the generation of them that seek him,
That seek thy face, O Jacob.
Lift up your heads, O ye gates;
And be ye lift up, ye everlasting doors;
And the King of glory shall come in . . .*

*As he reads, the lights dim slowly as the scene ends and the choir
is heard once more singing, "The Land is fair, the air is soft, etc."*

SCENE IV: *Hooker's Church in Newtown, now Cambridge, Massachusetts. October 8, 1635. At the left are seen* HAYNES, DUDLEY *and* WIN-
THROP. COTTON *and* HOOKER *are seated at the right in the first row of
pews.*

HAYNES *(turning and looking back, as if viewing the magistrates)*:
Mr. Dudley, are all our magistrates assembled?

DUDLEY:
They are here, already seated, Governor Haynes.
We are fifty magistrates and deputies, many weary
From their day-long travels to attend this General Court.

HAYNES *(to* WINTHROP*)*:
And the ministers we asked by special invitation?

WINTHROP *(pointing in the direction of* COTTON *and* HOOKER*)*:
They have arrived and are accounted in their seats.

HAYNES:
It is well. The added presence of
So many men of God must persuade Mr. Williams.
In these devout and honored souls he cannot help
But read his errors. Before we start the trial
I will talk with Mr. Hooker and Mr. Cotton.
  He walks down toward the congregation and HOOKER *and* COTTON
  rise to greet him.

DUDLEY *(to* WINTHROP*)*:
It is a cold day for October.
God grant we do not freeze before this trial ends.

WINTHROP:
Mr. Dudley, it is the cold of the soul
Crawling on the dirt floor of this church
That is on trial this day. If we freeze, Sir,
It is not our flesh from the frost of winter weather
But our souls for unjust persecution.

DUDLEY *(angered)*:
Do you call this solemn trial
Unjust before it has a start?

WINTHROP:
I speak only of our need to follow God's laws.
Much civil hatred has been raised against Mr. Williams
But he still has a strength of friends.

DUDLEY:

    This is the General Court and he shall speak
    Even if it be his toleration folly.
    I hope you do not judge this rebel minister
    Against the Bay because he was your friend.

WINTHROP:

    I will hear the arguments ... *(He turns away from* DUDLEY.*)*

HAYNES *(to* HOOKER*):*

    Mr. Hooker, we are many officers
    And bulge the walls of your small church,
    But we are grateful for your hospitality.

HOOKER:

    I am honored, Sir, to have my church
    As host to all the General Court,
    But shamed that Mr. Williams should be here on trial.

HAYNES:

    As are we all and trust that he will change
    When he does see the sacred weight and purpose
    Of our magistrates and men of God. *(turning to* COTTON*)*
    Mr. Cotton, it pleases me that
    You and all our ministers are present.
    It is a true and solemn meeting of God's will
    And I thank you for this plan
    To bring together ministers and magistrates.

COTTON:

    This unity of minds must sway his stubborn views,
    For he is a real danger, Sir. All people
    Speak for him on sight and do not see beneath his mask of love
    The Devil's swamp to which this toleration leads.

HAYNES:

    After I question him on the letters he did write
    Blocking our magistrates' authority and urging
    His Salem church to separate completely from our churches
    Of the Bay, I will ask Mr. Hooker to debate with him
    And as arranged you will also press the Charges.

COTTON:

As God calls us to fight all heresy

That His original Nation may revive again,

It is an onerous duty I cannot avoid.

HAYNES returns to his seat. COTTON *and* HOOKER *take their seats.*

HAYNES:

Let Mr. Williams know the Court is ready.

*The choir is heard singing softly "*DAVID THE KING.*"* WILLIAMS *enters.* HAYNES *motions him to the defendant's chair.*

HAYNES:

Before we begin the interrogation, Mr. Williams,

The members of the General Court have been disturbed

By your unwillingness to approve the authority

Of the Bay government. I would like first to ask

If you accept the responsibility and judgment of this Court.

WILLIAMS:

I do respect the members of this Court,

But it is by God's word only that I desire

To stand or fall in trial and judgment; for all flesh is grass

And the beauty of flesh is but the beauty of grass,

Only the word of God stands fast forever.

HAYNES:

You imply that members of the Court

Do not speak God's word on earth?

WILLIAMS:

I think, Sir, that man's wish is not always God's will.

DUDLEY:

By that indirection, do you mean

Your toleration of any cranks of God?

WINTHROP *(to* DUDLEY*):*

It was a fair answer. Let Governor Haynes proceed with the questions.

HAYNES:

Mr. Williams, do you deny writing this seditious letter

To all our churches in the Bay, *(showing the letter)*

40

Complaining of the magistrates
For their injustice to the Salem church?

WINTHROP:

I do deny the letter was seditious.

HAYNES:

But you admit the letter.

WILLIAMS:

The letter I have written protested the magistrates' rights
To refuse the petition of our Salem church
For land in Marblehead Neck only for the reason
That Salem refused to cast me out as teacher.
Is it just to punish Salem because of me?

HAYNES:

Did not the Salem congregation elect you as teacher
And were they not aware of the letter?

WILLIAMS:

They did join with me in the letter.

HAYNES:

Do you admit the letter accused
The lawful magistrates and deputies, in your own words,
Of a "heinous sin and a breach of the rule of justice"?

WILLIAMS:

Is it justice to bring about an action
By an inaction and by threats?

DUDLEY:

Look how he avoids commenting
On the hot-blooded words, "heinous sin."

WILLIAMS:

My language was perhaps too prideful but I do think
There was a sin of error against the Salem church.

DUDLEY:

So you begin your admission but retreat from it.

WINTHROP:

I do not believe we are here

41

To judge Mr. Williams's intemperate language.
It is the danger of his actions we must test.

DUDLEY:

Is not the letter an action, Mr. Winthrop?

HAYNES:

Let me proceed with the questioning.

WILLIAMS:

Before we turn from this point, Sir,
May I ask why the magistrates and elders
Refused to read our Salem letter
To their congregations? Were they afraid?

DUDLEY *(beside himself)*:

Is he to be permitted such insolence?

WINTHROP:

This is the General Court, Mr. Dudley.
We are not the Inquisition. Let Governor Haynes reply.

HAYNES:

We live in a young world of our Lord, Mr. Williams,
Surrounded by wilderness and heathen enemies of His word,
And so must enforce a central government in God's name
Lest petty camps of selfish gain destroy our faith.
Is your trust in the Salem congregation yet full?

WILLIAMS:

I think they are still my friends in God.

HAYNES:

But we have heard you are no longer
A teacher in the Salem church. Is this true?

WILLIAMS:

You know it is true. I have separated.

HAYNES:

Will you give us cause for this break?

WILLIAMS:

When the Salem church was threatened

The members decided to hold communion
With the churches of the Bay
And to accept the Marblehead Neck Land
That was in dispute. So I withdrew.

DUDLEY:

Threatened, you say, Mr. Williams, threatened!
This is abstract and general, Sir. Who did this threatening?

WILLIAMS:

I believe it was the magistrates of the Bay. *(General murmurs)*

DUDLEY:

You would accuse us directly? Has your pride no bounds?

WINTHROP:

Mr. Williams, it is a general and serious accusation.

HAYNES *(to* WILLIAMS*):*

By your own admission you have left your Salem church
And stand alone before this Court, accused
Even by your Salem friends . . . I wish to show you a second letter.
(He produces the letter) Do you deny this writing?

WILLIAMS:

No, it is my hand.

HAYNES:

This is a letter to your Salem church?

WILLIAMS:

It is.

HAYNES:

In which you seek to persuade your congregation
To renounce communion with all the churches in the Bay
As . . . "full of anti-Christian pollution"?
Are those your words, Sir?

WILLIAMS *(after a pause):*

They are my words, if my merit is not gentle writing.
I do not deny them. I have always believed in
The separation of the church from any national or popish organi-
zation.

43

DUDLEY *(enraged):*

You dare to call the Bay churches a Popish organization?

WINTHROP:

Gentlemen, we are not here to argue
The organization of the Bay churches against the Salem church.
Let us present the specific charges against Mr. Williams.

HAYNES:

Since the letters have been acknowledged I should like
First to give Mr. Williams a final chance to recant them.

WINTHROP:

Mr. Williams, will you reconsider the spirit of your letters?
Revenge is not our purpose in this Court.

WILLIAMS:

I do not deny a sinful pride
That I work against in my person,
But I cannot recant the spirit of my letters.

DUDLEY:

What shall we do with a pride that condemns
And prompts itself all in a locked unison?

WINTHROP:

I can accept it, Mr. Dudley. Have you never felt it?

HAYNES:

Please, Sirs, I ask Mr. Winthrop to read the specific Charges.
Then I will appoint the arguer of the Charges.

WINTHROP *(reading):* "On this eighth day of October, in the year of
our Lord, 1635, the General Court of Massachusetts, meeting in
solemn session, does present the following Charges against Mr. Roger
Williams of Salem:

First, that Mr. Williams has constantly rebuked the churches of
Massachusetts Bay for not abjuring all connection with the Church
of England.

Second, that Mr. Williams has disputed, refused to sign, and con-
tended against the Resident's Oath of Fidelity which the magistrates
had ordered for safeguard of the colony.

44

Third, that Mr. Williams has contested the validity of the charter of Massachusetts, granted to the colony by the King's hand.

Fourth, that Mr. Williams has declared that the civil magistrates of the Bay have not the power to punish breaches of the First Table of the Decalogue.

HAYNES:

You have heard the Charges, Mr. Williams,
Drawn up by the fifty members of this Court
And attested by our ministers whom we have invited here.
You will be given your chance to answer.
The Court has asked our honored minister,
Mr. Thomas Hooker, to debate with you.
The Court has also requested our learned Man of God,
Mr. John Cotton, to speak. I do think you will listen to them
Since you have known them to speak the Lord's word.

WILLIAMS:

I respect them and desire that my rejoinders
Shall be as full of love as truth.

DUDLEY:

A mixed figure again, pricked with pride.

WINTHROP:

Let Mr. Hooker and Mr. Cotton debate with him, and he must change
By the force of their gift. They are distinguished speakers.

HAYNES:

Mr. Hooker will begin with the First Charge.

HOOKER *(rises):*

In the First Charge, the issue is one of separation,
Whether our Bay churches shall be secure and centrally organized
Or split off completely from the Church of England.
I do not think Mr. Williams will now accuse me
Of a friendship with the English church under King Charles.
He remembers well how Archbishop Laud suppressed my lectureship
And drove me from the land on pain of death. It was the gilded
English hierarchy, kin to the tyrannical structure of Rome,
Where no man could speak himself to God and

45

The voices of the congregation sank into a whisper,
That Mr. Williams, Mr. Cotton and myself did suffer from.
I ask Mr. Williams if he recalls the day of exile
When we three ministers rode together from our homes
Fleeing the Courts of Injustice for this new world?

WILLIAMS:

I do remember and honor that day of our friendship
And persuasion against the national church when it was
Bitter as death to me that Bishop Laud pursued us out of the land.

WINTHROP *(to* HAYNES*):*

It is well. He will be persuaded.

HOOKER:

Here in this green harbor of the Bay we began anew
The eternal task of salvation, surrounded by all perils
Of the wilderness and of the hidden, heathen savages;
And we considered gratefully God's words:

"This is the token of the covenant which I make between me and
you and every living creature that is with you, for perpetual gen-
erations: I do set my bow in the cloud, and when the bow shall
be seen in that cloud, I will remember my covenant, and the waters
shall no more become a flood to destroy all flesh."

It is God's bow we have seen in this clouded land
Commanding us to remember this eternal covenant,
And to unite forever the church and state.
In our congregations we have exercised a new freedom
And given them the privilege of election which belongs
To the people according to the blessed will and
Lasting law of God. But if we separate from our
English mother church and stifle the growth of
Our theocratic state, we cast aside all hope
Of law and unity, of peaceful growth in God's new land.
Turning directly to WILLIAMS.
I pray with you, good friend, let not
This colony of Massachusetts be like that sheet
Let down from heaven, clung to by beasts and
Creeping things, but let it be a Garden of the Lord. *(He sits down.)*

DUDLEY:
He cannot refute this gift of tongue!

WINTHROP:
It is well-spoken.

HAYNES:
Mr. Williams, what is your consideration of these words?

WILLIAMS:
Mr. Hooker has spoken well of God's covenant to Noah,
But I remind him of the Tower of Babel where God said:

> "Behold, the people is one, and they have all one language; and this
> they begin to do; and now nothing will be restrained from them,
> which they have imagined to do. Go to, let us go down, and there
> confound their language, that they may not understand one an-
> other's speech."

And therefore was the language of all men confounded
As a warning to man's soul from the Lord. I do not believe
The Old Testament can be read in a complete and solemn literalness.
It is figures, stories of God's will, and if you seek
To build from it again a nation modeled after ancient Israel
Such a thing can never come to pass. The Lord did
Scatter men upon the face of earth that in their lonely lives
They would seek God's grace and never build again a unity of church
and state.

DUDLEY:
It is heresy to take the Bible as mere figures!

HAYNES:
What does Mr. Cotton say to this?

COTTON:
For myself I find it sinful to take God's words
As anything but sense. Does not Mr. Williams remember
The honored Calvin's saying on those who speak of stories in the
    Bible:
"It is better to confess ignorance than to play with frivolous guesses"?

47

WILLIAMS:

    I have read the learned Calvin's words,
    But I do think that in the heart of man
    We live by figures of good and evil;
    And that when the witnesses of Jesus Christ
    Have opened a gap in the wall of separation
    Between the garden of the church and the wilderness of the world,
    God has ever broken down the wall and made His garden a wilderness
      again.
    The word of God cannot be shown clearly by the strictures of
    A national church lest every conscience be forced into a soul-rape.

DUDLEY:

    Soul-rape indeed!

HAYNES:

    You have spoken on the First Charge, Mr. Williams,
    And we hear your words of passion with regret.
    I ask Mr. Cotton to speak on the Second Charge.

COTTON *(he stands):*

    The Second Charge concerns the Resident's Oath of Fidelity
    Requested by the magistrates to insure due loyalty to God
    And to all lawful functions of the Bay authorities.
    This oath did arise upon hearing of some episcopal
    And malignant practices against the colony, when the magistrates
    And others of the General Court thought meet to take a trial
    Of the people's faith. In case any should refuse to sign the oath
    They would not be elected to public command.
    None can say that oaths are novel to this colony;
    In early times men swore by sacred rivers,
    The Jew swore with his sacred scrolls in his hand,
    Doctors have always taken oaths to cure
    And clergymen have read their solemn oaths of ordination.
    In our mother England the practice of
    Kissing the Good Book and swearing arose in the Middle Ages.
    An oath is but a sign of man's allegiance to the Lord.

WILLIAMS *(rising):*

    I am not as versed in history of oaths

As is the honored scholar, Mr. Cotton,
But I do agree that oaths are not a universal evil.
It is often just that men should swear to do God's will.

COTTON:

Why then is it unjust that the Bay in time of growing need,
As security from savages and disloyal men,
Should demand allegiance to the ways of God?

WILLIAMS:

Because it is an oath of force and not of choice.
You would have every boy of sixteen years
And every man above that age within the Bay
Speak and sign that tight and lengthy oath.
Is this an act of freedom?

COTTON:

I fear, Sir, you will not face the facts.
We are few men within this narrow Bay
And ringed around by many heathen Indians.
If we do not command obedience to our church
How will this colony survive?

WILLIAMS:

If it is God's will, it will survive,
As rule by man's will alone will perish.
Since that first fall from the immortal Garden,
Religion is no longer the clear waters of God in which
Man swims toward the light, but a muddy surface
Armed with a fin which razors towards the soul.

COTTON:

Sir, this oath I think is not a razor. I bid you
Not become a haberdasher of small questions.

WILLIAMS:

Many questions, Mr. Cotton, for the Lord
Suit better than a lack of change into His mercy.

COTTON:

This is splinters, Mr. Williams, splinters.
Can you not give us clearer cause against the oath?

49

WILLIAMS:

  An oath is but an act of worship and prayer,
  An image of trust wrung freely from a loyal soul.
  It does profane both acts of worship and of prayer
  To force an oath on one whose lips it sounds
  False and sinful. In *Matthew* and in *James*
  Christ counsels, "Swear not at all."
  If we consider this wise injunction,
  Then we must fear the nature of false oaths.
  An oath, being an invocation of God's truth, is
  An action of deep spirit and religious nature.
  Christian men ought not to take an oath
  Merely to maintain mortal men in offices of power.

WINTHROP:

  I think he speaks as many men agree.

DUDLEY:

  He is contesting at us magistrates.

HAYNES:

  Mr. Williams, you will not change upon this oath?

WILLIAMS:

  I have not been persuaded.

HAYNES:

  I beg you consider, Sir, the time is late.
  We have honored your reputation and long tolerated your dissent.
  I beg you think if the honored names here gathered
  In this Newtown church speak nothing more than air to you.

WILLIAMS:

  Sir, I listen to your charges with respect,
  When you are many voices to my one.

HAYNES:

  Let Mr. Hooker speak upon the Third Charge.

HOOKER *(he stands)*:

  In the Third Charge, it is the claim of Mr. Williams
  That the Charter of our Bay, granted by the King,

Gives us no legal right to own the land.
For this puzzle I have no statement but a question.
We are a people of God in what was once the Devil's territory.
Would Mr. Williams have us depart
And leave God's new land to the savages?

DUDLEY:

He is a haberdasher and cannot wriggle from that point.

WILLIAMS:

How can we leave the land to the Indians
When they were here before our ships arrived?
I have heard the men of this court speak of
The danger of savages and the security of this colony of God.
I know what it is to study, to preach, to be an elder,
To be applauded — and yet also what it is to tug at the oar
And dig with the spade in rocky soil, to plow and labor
And travel by day and night amongst English and those you call
  Devils.
I have earned my family's food by barter with the Indians
And have seen the same sun shine on the wilderness as does
Shine upon the order of a garden. In that wilderness
How sweetly did I hear the several sorts of heaven's birds
Sing unto men the soaring praise of their maker's wisdom and good-
  ness;
And to me the wilderness was a clear resemblance of the world
Where greedy and furious men persecute and devour the hinds and
  roes.

DUDLEY:

There bloom his figures again.

WINTHROP:

Mr. Hooker will answer him.

HOOKER:

We have heard you have forsaken your minister's career
For trade with the Indians. Do you consider it
Just and truthful that those called by God
Should learn and follow the ways of savages?

51

WILLIAMS:

Your inference is that my time is lost
Because not in the function of ministry.
I admit the offices of Christ are the sacred
And best callings, but generally they are the worst trades
As they are practiced only for a maintenance,
A place, a living, a benefice.

WINTHROP:

That is twist for turn.

HOOKER:

You confess, then, that you trade with savages
And make no effort to bring them to God's word?

WILLIAMS:

I spoke no confession. A great will can convert
Many men, but the convert through will power
Belongs to the will and not to God.

HOOKER:

Sir, if it is right you trade with Indians,
Why can we not minister to our Charter?

WILLIAMS:

Because as God's children we know the world lies in wickedness,
A sea of wild beasts, and God is over this wild, foaming world,
Over the heathen Indians as well as Christians.
Where have you gained this Charter? From the Indians
Who had the land before a ship sailed into port,
Or from the King who never did set foot on it?

HOOKER:

Do I understand, Sir, you believe a Christian King
Cannot give title to a savage land
In God's name and for God's sacred word?

WILLIAMS:

I do contend the land was seized and sanctioned
By the King. There was no purchase from the Indians.

HOOKER:

Mr. Williams, you have spoken against oaths,

Saying unregenerate men cannot swear.
How then can a savage swear away a land by purchase?
Would not such acts blaspheme against the Lord?

WILLIAMS:

I have lived much with these Indians.
My soul's desire was to do them good
And God was pleased to give me a powerful, patient spirit
To lodge with them in their filthy, smoky holes
To gain their tongue. They have no clothes, books nor letters
And therefore are easily persuaded
That the God who made Englishmen is a greater God
Because He has endowed the English greater than themselves.
And yet amongst their government and justice
I could never discern that scandalous excess of sins
With which old Europe does abound. Is it just then to
Strike them with the civil sword and seize their lands?

HOOKER:

You have slipped my question, Sir.
How can a savage swear to a purchase?

WILLIAMS:

It is not the savage who must swear
But the Christian bound to God's word. I wish to say
That what you are trying in me here is a desire,
A desire more perfect than human actions,
More beautiful than human aims,
A desire for the clarity of God's grace.

WINTHROP:

It is too perfect.

WILLIAMS:

I do not think that search for Christian grace can come
From smiting and killing savages, but only from
The patient aim to bear and carry the cross and gallows
Of our Lord and patiently to suffer with Him.

HOOKER:

Mr. Williams, we live in a new wilderness

And the Lord descends on this land as He descended
In fire on Moses atop Mount Sinai. Then you remember
There were thunder and lightnings and a thick cloud
Upon the mount and the voice of the trumpet exceeding loud
So that all the people in the camp trembled.
This is the state of this colony in the Bay, Sir,
And the Lord calls us as He called to Moses:
   "Thou shalt have no other Gods before me. Thou shalt not make
   unto thee any graven image ... for I the Lord am a jealous God
   visiting the iniquity of the fathers upon the children ..."
This is a strict God for heathens, Mr. Williams.
He commands our absolute faith and devotion
And will punish ourselves if we deal with savages.

DUDLEY:
   This word cannot be denied.

HAYNES *(to* WILLIAMS*):*
   Sir, you have a last chance to refute this sense.

WILLIAMS:
   I do speak against the bloody tenet of persecution for cause of con
      science,
   That forces men to use the sword in cause of Christ,
   A tenet of high blasphemy against the Lord of peace who said,
   "Blessed are the peacemakers for they shall be called the children o
      God,"
   A tenet fighting the sweet end of Christ's coming which was
   Not to destroy men's lives for their religions, but to save them;
   A tenet against which the blessed souls under the altar
   Cry aloud for vengeance, this tenet having cut their throats,
   Torn out their hearts, and poured forth their blood in all ages;
   A tenet which no uncleanness, no adultery, no incest,
   Sodomy, or bestiality can equal — this ravishment and
   Forcing of souls and conscience throughout the world.
   I say to this Court this bloody tenet kindles the devouring flames o
      war
   And is mingled with the murders and poisonings of kings and states.
   If we do force the nature of the Prince of Peace against these
      heathens

54

We are that stiff-necked people whom the Lord accused to Moses.
The Christian church does not prosecute, no more than a lily
Does scratch the thorns, or a lamb pursue and tear the wolves.

HAYNES:

Sir, we have permitted you to counter our General Court
With lengthy passion, but this I must ask Mr. Cotton to refute.

COTTON:

I will not exercise a vanity of pride.
It is enough to speak the conscience of this Court,
Our fifty magistrates and many ministers
Who speak this colony's God-humbled will.
Like Moses, we live in a new world of God,
A new land of Israel, to war against idolaters,
And in this war we speak the prayer of peace
But carry a sword to defend ourselves and homes.
It is the will of God, His truth,
Never to kill or banish any for conscience,
But this Court speaking in God's name
Has the right and duty to punish those
Who sin against their own true conscience
Whether from pride, or other commandments of the Lord.

HAYNES:

Mr. Williams has been refuted. If any officer
Will add his thoughts I ask him now to speak. *(There is a tense
    silence.)*
Mr. Cotton will present the final Charge.

COTTON:

In the Fourth Charge, Mr. Williams declares steadfastly
That the Civil Magistrate may not punish
Breaches of the First Table of the Decalogue
And declares us in danger of setting up a national church
For that we punish breaches of this Table.
It is his view that commandments in the First Table
Pertain to man's duties to the Lord
And therefore cannot be punished by civil officers.
But it is my view that our congregational system,

Wherein each member of the church can freely voice God's word,
Requires for its maintenance a vigorous magistracy.
These magistrates are elders of the church and
Therefore strong-willed men of God. Does Mr. Williams think
Such men likely to rule against the Lord?

WILLIAMS:

Within this church and Court we speak upon the Bible's word,
But all of you, I think, do know and praise the words of Luther
When he said: "The laws of the civil magistrate's government extend
  no further than over the body and goods and that which is external;
  for over the Soul God will not suffer any man to rule."

COTTON:

It is a special situation, Sir.
Many of the civil magistrates whom Luther fought were
Bound to Rome. In a wild and savage country like this Bay
The foundation of the civil power must lie
In magistrates who do God's will, else must the heathen dancers
Prance once more around their Calf of Gold.

WILLIAMS:

You always harken back to ancient Israel,
A blessed nation dead in time. That wrath
And glory of God cannot ever be revived.

COTTON:

Must all states then be secular?
How would you guide this youthful land,
Open it wide to enemies of the church?

WILLIAMS:

I think the wilderness of every land is like the sea.
Out on this sullen sea goes many a ship
Crammed with hundreds of hungry souls,
Each with his own crude, common woes
And so this ship is like a commonwealth;
Upon it, sometimes, live both Turk and Jew,
Papist and Protestant, in common perils
And no one forces them together for ship's prayers.
Each prays according to his worth and need.

56

COTTON:

A soul-saving ship? You are a most
Prodigious minter of exorbitant novelties.
And who may rule this ship?

WILLIAMS:

I have never denied the ship's commander
Should command the ship's true course
And rule that peace and justice shall be kept.
If any seaman dare refuse his duty,
Or any passenger conceive a lawless deed,
The laws and orders of the ship should punish him.
But for the hungry souls that pray to God,
Within the private chambers of their hearts
This ship sails true to each man's prayer.

COTTON:

It is a sinking ship where each man drowns at a false altar.

WINTHROP:

I think it is a separation we once did believe ourselves.

DUDLEY:

All he does is contend against the magistrates.
Question him on this finally.

COTTON:

Mr. Williams, I have pleaded with you many times,
For days before the meeting of this Court
And now within this solemn session
To persuade you from your pride's delusion.
If the magistrates fail to rule for God
Pagan anarchy will rule and then, Sir,
We shall see new tables of stone
Engraved with the terrible fiery finger of the Lord.

WILLIAMS:

The name of Christian must deserve the name.
Constantine and all the noted emperors are confessed to have done
More hurt to the crown of Christ than did the bloody Neros.
I say again the forcing of conscience is a rape of soul!

57

The civil sword may make a nation of hypocrites
And anti-Christians, but not one Christian.

DUDLEY:

He calls us hypocrites!

WINTHROP:

Ask him to recall.

HAYNES:

Question him on this.

COTTON *(to* WILLIAMS*):*

Sir, do you name our magistrates hypocrites?

WILLIAMS:

I call that man a hypocrite who thinks the civil sword,
Bloodied in God's name, will make a Christian world.
And I desire Mr. Cotton and every soul in this Court
Seriously to consider if the Lord Jesus were himself in person,
In old or in this New England, what church, what ministry.
What government, He would set up, and what prosecution
He would practice toward them that would not receive Him?

HAYNES:

We have spoken patiently with you for long hours, Mr. Williams,
And have not silenced the pride of your tongue
Although you speak as one dissent against the word of
Many Godly men. We give you a last chance to recant these Charges.

WILLIAMS:

I will not recant these Charges. Whatever fate I suffer
It is but a shadow vanished. Eternity will pay for all.

WINTHROP:

He has spoken his fate.

HAYNES:

The hearing is concluded for today.
Mr. Williams, you will return tomorrow morning
For the judgment of this General Court. (WILLIAMS *goes out.*)

DUDLEY *(vehemently, as the members of the Court begin their deliberation):*

I say let men of God in court and churches watch
O'er such as do a toleration hatch!
The lights fade out as the scene ends and the choir is heard singing,
WONDROUS LOVE.

EPILOGUE

SCENE V: *As the lights go up, Governor Haynes is about to deliver the verdict to Williams.*

HAYNES: On this morning of our Lord, October 9, 1635, the General Court of Massachusetts, meeting in solemn session, does find you, Roger Williams of Salem, unpersuaded after many hours of the Lord's arguments as humbly submitted by magistrates and ministers of His Bay Colony. Therefore, the General Court does find you guilty as **charged of the** following points: First, persisting and preaching the false doctrine that the Churches of the Bay should profess separation. Second, denying that a magistrate can tender an oath of Civil Obedience to all men of the Bay. Third, falsely declaring that the Royal Charter fails to give the Colony a valid title to the land of New England. Fourth, asserting that the magistrates in whom resides the civil authority should not punish breaches of the first four Commandments. It is the judgment of this General Court that . . .

MAN'S VOICE: Wait!
The figures of the Court suddenly become stylized and stiff as if frozen in time. They hold these poses until Haynes completes the sentence at the end of the Epilogue. The lights dim around them and two figures in modern clothes become apparent, the JOURNALIST *and the* EVANGELIST, *who are dressed as they were in the Prologue.*

WILLIAMS:
Who are you? What do you want? Why has the trial stopped?

JOURNALIST:
The trial hasn't stopped. It will conclude presently.

EVANGELIST:
We've come to show you the glorious past of Roger Williams!

WILLIAMS:

Why should I listen to you?

JOURNALIST:

But I'm not a devil, only a journalist,
A historian of religion. I've studied the past of Roger Williams.

WILLIAMS:

The pursuit of the past is a passion of death.

JOURNALIST:

My study of the past is your future.

WILLIAMS:

I care only for the future salvation of man's soul.

JOURNALIST:

My dear Sir, I can't give you any kind of view
Of *the* future. No man sees that sort of thing.

EVANGELIST *(to* WILLIAMS *while she scorns the* JOURNALIST*):*
Don't listen to his cynical mind.
You've liberated the church from the state's tyranny.
I can show you the glory of your own radiant progress . . .

JOURNALIST:

She's only an evangelist. Let me begin . . .

WILLIAMS *(troubled, he speaks finally to the* JOURNALIST*):*
My love is for the truth of God, and peace of conscience.
If you can bring me that peace, begin . . .

JOURNALIST *(waving aside the* EVANGELIST *triumphantly):*
I bring you the peace of History. This is 1958,
More than 350 years after your birth. You were born
At the end of the Elizabethan age when a great culture was dying.

WILLIAMS:

I do not know what you mean by culture.
I believed only in the search for God.

JOURNALIST:

That's the irony of it, Mr. Williams.
After all these years you've been

Taken over by this Evangelist and other fanatics.
Your heresy has become heroic
Under the ironic name of religious freedom.

EVANGELIST:
Don't listen to him!

WILLIAMS *(slowly)*:
I always dreamt of religious freedom
For all churches in the wilderness of the world.

JOURNALIST:
Men have twisted your ideal of religious freedom
And spoken of you as the precursor of Jeffersonian democracy,
A founder of liberalism and rationalism,
One of the makers of political freedom.

WILLIAMS:
I never was a politician. I hated politics.
My only belief was in the heaven of God
And the search for God in man's soul.

EVANGELIST *(crying out)*:
That is my belief too!

JOURNALIST *(mocking her)*:
In History the Devil's question is not
"Where is God?" but "What is the human church?"

WILLIAMS:
Some men think the church an altar
To expose the sacred mystery of our Lord,
Where forever the longing of the heart
May be stilled in the blessing of its need;
While other men think of the church as God's word
Sounding through a humble minister's voice
Until the word of love lights up the sacred hall.

JOURNALIST:
But you never thought of the church in these ways.
In History men call you a Seeker.

61

WILLIAMS:

That is true. To me the human church is but
A house of error and of search and all men in it,
Catholic, Protestant, or Jew, kneel there as eternal Seekers;
For it is written: "Seek and ye shall find,"
And what man finds is in the seeking,
In the peril and pilgrimage of search
Lies his only reward and salvation,
Never to know on earth the light of paradise,
But only a knowledge of suffering,
Of the inseparable knots of hate and love.

EVANGELIST *(radiantly)*:

That is the meaning of faith.

JOURNALIST *(ironically)*:

That is the peace of History
In which you have found your high place.

WILLIAMS *(to the* JOURNALIST*)*:

Your history is only proof of the world's wilderness.
The peace of the true Seeker of God does not come
From knocking at the door of time,
But from knocking at the soul's timeless door . . .

JOURNALIST:

You have knocked at the door of time.
    As WILLIAMS *stares at him, the* EVANGELIST *moves impatiently in*
    front of the JOURNALIST*.)*

EVANGELIST:

Do not despair, Roger Williams, at men of little faith.
Christ must return in blazing light
And the Seeker nears the end of his search.
His history only sweats in the record of fleshly lust *(She is scorning*
    the JOURNALIST*)*   ;
But I can tell you of the soul's progress
And of man's longing steps toward God.

JOURNALIST:

She'll tell you sentimental lies.

WILLIAMS *(after a moment of hesitation, to the* EVANGELIST*)*:
Perhaps you are my truth. I will listen to you.

EVANGELIST *(from this point on, the fire of her voice increases)*:
I bring you good tidings of a joyous God, from a time
When churches blaze over His green land and the sky is
Brilliant white with neon-lighted crosses to His name.

WILLIAMS *(uncertain)*:
The joy of God is not the joy of man.

EVANGELIST:
Now God builds the innocent church and scorches
The guilty preacher with the power of His radiation.

JOURNALIST:
Her radiation means death today.

WILLIAMS *(to the* EVANGELIST*)*:
How did you find His power of salvation?

EVANGELIST:
One night in the darkness of my room,
Poor and sick in a factory city, a dazzling light
Scarred the wall and the burning voice of His radiation
Spoke from the scorched plaster:"Wherefore seek ye not
    redemption?"

WILLIAMS:
What did you learn from this voice?

EVANGELIST:
The Lord healed me with His mercy, and I went into the world
To preach God's glory which
I call the Gospel of Radiant Redemption.

WILLIAMS:
Which you call or which God calls?
Are you my truth or my false pride?

JOURNALIST *(scornfully)*:
This is the History which your pride has created.

EVANGELIST *(ecstatically)*:
I feel His light every Sunday at my Sacred Radiation Service,

63

When I walk down the silver staircase and the spotlight
Flashes on the golden altar underneath the voice of the choir—
Then I feel His radiance burning through me,
Commanding me to preach His Gospel!

WILLIAMS:
A silver staircase and a golden altar as His Truth?
God commands no one to preach in vanity.
What proof have you of His will?

EVANGELIST:
Here, I give you charts of all our American churches, *(She does so*
Old and new, who have separated from the state
To create fresh hymns of glory as you willed.

WILLIAMS *(looking doubtfully at the charts):*
So many churches ... These may be splinters of the
Devil's will. *(He pushes them away)*

JOURNALIST *(to* WILLIAMS*):*
You have created them yourself.

EVANGELIST:
In your name new religions of Jesus spread their
Warming currents and the air is charged with miracles of hope.
God is a power like radiation to consume the body with joy
And devour the evil mind into an ash of burning terror!

WILLIAMS *(tormented):*
I am that evil mind.

EVANGELIST:
Blessings on you, Roger Williams,
You have shown us the radiance of Jesus.

WILLIAMS:
I have shown you nothing.

JOURNALIST:
You have shown us the fate of History.

WILLIAMS:
My faith is not in the time of your History.

64

EVANGELIST:
You have shown us the simplicity of God
And the freedom of His eternal love.

WILLIAMS:
The danger of simplicity is always tyranny,
Of reducing the mystery of God's love
To the greed of man's love for power.

EVANGELIST *(in a last, ecstatic outburst, she pushes in front of the*
JOURNALIST*):*
His radiation and simplicity! Blessings on you, Roger Williams.
Praise the Lord! Praise His name, His peace, His everlasting love,
His Love! . . .

The lights go up abruptly and the figures of the JOURNALIST *and*
the EVANGELIST *disappear. Just after the echo of the* EVANGELIST'S
last fervent cry of "Love!", the frozen pose of Governor Haynes
relaxes and he completes the verdict.

HAYNES: . . . the hateful errors of pride must be driven from this new
land of God. Therefore, the General Court of Massachusetts Bay,
respecting and humbly praising His divine mercy, sentences you to
immediate and eternal banishment. On pain of death you will never
again be permitted to live within the boundaries of this colony. Is
there anything final you wish to say?

WILLIAMS *(turning away from the members of the Court):*
I will not answer you for my own pride.
This Court has found in me false images,
But no more than I have found in myself.
In my need I have heard the word of God
That men distort in their bloody tenet
Of persecution for cause of conscience.
I have seen the acts of murder and war
Men commit in the name of the Prince of Peace.
I have felt the dangerous heresy of a future
When the cure of love is cried in false simplicity
And the material stones of life are called divine.
I know the common trinity of the world is

65

Profit, preferment, and pleasure—but still I believe
That the human weeds in the Lord's garden must be left
To His judgment; the music of God sings above man's bloody laws,
The choir begins to sing softly the last stanza of "WONDROUS LOVE"
A music of the regal senses
Rising above a tyrant's rules of order.
Sometimes, this music seems disorder,
A luring echo of magical sounds,
And then we damn it with the name of Devil,
The fallen angel from the brillant air.
Our danger then is that we damn all music
Until the rigid rules harden to hate.
In one moment God may reach us,
A moment of utter timelessness,
Yet we may reach God only through
An agony of separation from His love.
And so I pray against my pride and yours—
Oh Lord, let Thy music sing in the winter of man's exile!
After Williams finishes speaking, the choir repeats, full-voice this
time, the last stanza of "WONDROUS LOVE":

> *And when from death I'm free*
> *I'll sing and joyful be*
> *And through eternity,*
> *I'll sing on, I'll sing on,*
> *And through eternity*
> *I'll sing on.*

American
Power

Two Related One Act Plays

To Eric Bentley

THE SPACE FAN: A Play of Escape

The setting is a shed in the backyard of Melinda Davis, a space fan. A clutter of unorthodox space equipment is scattered throughout the shed. The chief item of equipment is a large, home-made space panel with switches and knobs that dominates the center of the stage. A roll of tape protrudes from the left side of the panel. As the play begins, Melinda is pacing up and down in front of the panel. The crackling of a space message is heard, high and eerie music. Melinda begins to rush back and forth adjusting various pieces of equipment. An interfering voice is heard over one recalcitrant piece of equipment, "Charlie, you green? Will you pick up an old lady at the corner of Fourth and Main?" She bangs the piece of equipment impatiently and the voice stops abruptly. Melinda is middle-aged, fantastic, plain-spinsterish, intense, definitely tuned into space. She is dressed in a cap, a colorful jacket, slacks, and tennis shoes. As the crackling of the space message is heard more intensely she rushes to the space panel and picks up a home-made microphone.)

MELINDA *(Excited and blissful):*

Friendship I... Friendship I... Come in, please... All systems go
Commander? ... Roger. Reading you clearly... Approaching Cali
fornia coast... Second orbit... (She pulls off a piece of tape from
the space panel, looks at it, and crumples it up.) Deploy balloon for
drag experiment. ... Inflating... Up, up... Thirty inches, beach
ball size! ... How's the resistance? None? ... Wonderful space..
No resistance... Have you exercised yet? ... Still flying by wire
... Careful... Not too long... Don't get cocky in your barber chair
... You'll fall behind in your experiments... You guys all want to
wobble the stick... That's where the fuel goes... Try your exer
cises... The one with the thick rubber band... *(She stretches an
imaginary rubber band.)* How's the temperature in your suit?...Up
two degrees? ... Watch it! *(She checks anxiously on a piece of
equipment.)* Stop using your rubber exerciser. Drink plenty of
water! ... *(She drinks.)* Any trouble drinking? ... Good... Try
some food!... *(She eats.)* Squeeze it slowly out of the tube..
Check pressure in the capsule... Look for the creeps!... Over Africa
now. ... You'll hit Spain in a minute... Get ready for your Spanish
broadcast... *(A touch of Spanish music is heard through the space
sounds and her feet kick out instinctively into a dance for a moment
Then she rushes to the side of the stage, picks up a long speaking tube
and calls out.)* Ground stations, stand by! *(She turns back to the
microphone.)* Fuel consumption is excessive... Watch it. ... Fly
manual control... What's the matter? ... You sound tired... Can't
read you... Come in, Commander, come in! ... *(Then, with relief
What were you doing?... Photographing the cloud cover... Beauti
ful, huh.. You've never seen anything like it... Approaching Cali
fornia coast, final orbit... You've done it, Commander! That's it
(She lets out a cheer.) Ground stations standing by to fire retro
rockets... You're not going to use the automatic system?... It's up
to you... You'll fly the capsule into position by manual and fly-by
wire? ... You're sure you can do it? You know how it wobbles..
(More and more excited) Check tilt!... Thirty-four degree angle
to horizon... *(She checks on a slide rule and leans into the required
angle.)* Right... Ready?... Ignite retro rockets! *(Then, worried
What's wrong? ... Damn, they're late!... Fire!... 1 - 2 - 3 - 4 - 5
... There... Thank God... *(Still alarmed)* Five seconds late..

Can't hear you any more ... Re-entry heat's blacked you out ... Call-ing Recovery Ship headquarters ... Recovery Ship headquarters ... Retro rockets fired five seconds late ... Angle of re-entry smaller ... Space ship may land far beyond target area ... Prepare para-medical units! Friendship I ... Friendship I ... Do you read me? ... Come in, Commander ... Wow, what happened to you? ... God, that was a real cliffhanger ... *(Still listening, she begins to laugh with relief. After the excitement, she sags into a chair downstage. The Investi-gator, reserved, dogged in steel-rimmed glasses, dressed in a con-servative suit and hat, enters and approaches her.)*

INVESTIGATOR:
Excuse me ...

MELINDA *(Still excited, hardly conscious of him):*
He's down safely and floating in the tub.

INVESTIGATOR:
The tub?

MELINDA:
The raft in the sea ...
    (Then, surprised)
What are you doing here?

INVESTIGATOR:
Are you Miss Melinda Davis?

MELINDA:
Yes ...

INVESTIGATOR *(Showing her his indentification card and then putting it away):*
I'd like to ask you a few questions if you don't mind ...

MELINDA:
I don't mind ... Who are you?
    (The Investigator pulls out his indentification card again and she reads.)
"William Reynolds ... The Bureau of Space Areonautics."
You're an investigator?

INVESTIGATOR:
Yes.

69

MELINDA *(Looking more closely at his photo on the identification card)*
It's not a very good likeness ... What can I do for you?

INVESTIGATOR *(Looking around at the cluttered equipment)*:
We've been having some trouble with interference on restricte
frequencies.

MELINDA:
That's a shame.

INVESTIGATOR:
Some interference perhaps from your equipment. *(He stumbles a littl
over a piece of equipment.)*

MELINDA:
Oh, I don't believe in interference.

INVESTIGATOR *(Looking around)*:
I see ... What are you doing with all this equipment?

MELINDA:
Listening.

INVESTIGATOR:
Listening? To what?

MELINDA:
To space.

INVESTIGATOR:
What do you hear in space?

MELINDA:
Messages.

INVESTIGATOR:
What kind of messages?

MELINDA:
A new language of sounds and music.

INVESTIGATOR *(Suspiciously)*:
You mean like a code?

MELINDA:
I suppose you could call it that. It has its own secrets, its distances.

70

INVESTIGATOR (*Crossing to a table and opening his briefcase*):

I'd like to ask you some personal questions ...(*She helps him out by cleaning various papers and books off the top of the table. Then she picks up a bottle of vodka and offers him a drink.*)

MELINDA:

Would you have a little Vodka?

INVESTIGATOR (*Stiffly*):

No thanks ... Not when I'm working. (*Melinda pours herself a drink. The Investigator fumbles around in his briefcase, disclosing his unfamiliarity with the job. Finally, he pulls out a piece of paper.*) You were born in Canton, Ohio, the only child of a physician, Dr. Ralph Davis ... Your father was all right, member of the Rotary Club, International Order of Odd Fellows ...

MELINDA:

Yes, he was the secretary ...

INVESTIGATOR (*Continuing*):

In high school you were something of a prodigy and won all sorts of prizes in Mathematics, Trig ... It's kind of blurred ...

MELINDA:

Trigonometry ... There was no competition then ...

INVESTIGATOR:

You won a scholarship to the University of Chicago ... (*Looking at the record*) Sciences, Humanities ... There's no record of your graduating.

MELINDA:

I never believed in graduating, just studying.

INVESTIGATOR:

How many years did you study?

MELINDA:

Ages, happy ages.

INVESTIGATOR (*Looking at the record*):

You studied Russian and other foreign languages in addition to the sciences ...

MELINDA:

I was a dabbler in everything I'm afraid.

INVESTIGATOR:

After college you became an exchange student. France, Italy, Greece Russia . . .

MELINDA:

Greece was lovely . . .

INVESTIGATOR:

What were you doing in Russia?

MELINDA:

I wasn't a student there really, just traveling. I went to see the place where Pushkin died.

INVESTIGATOR:

Pushkin?

MELINDA:

The poet. He was an impulsive, handsome young man, part Negro, the idol of the Tsar's court. He married a beautiful, vain woman who had many admirers. Pushkin was terribly jealous. He discovered that his wife was having an affair. He slapped the offender with his glove and challenged him to a duel. Weapons, pistols, were selected. That morning, as the sun rose through the white birch trees outside of St. Petersburg, Pushkin drove in his carriage to the appointed place. Back to back with his enemy, pistols up, they paced off ten steps, turned and fired!

INVESTIGATOR *(Trying to restrain himself but he can't):*
Pushkin was killed!

MELINDA:

Yes, it created a terrible scandal in the court. All of St. Petersburg turned out for the funeral. People were crying in the streets and reciting Pushkin's verses . . . *(She recites a couple of lines of Pushkin's poetry and toasts Pushkin with her glass.)*

INVESTIGATOR *(Trying to get back to the subject):*
I see . . . When you came back you worked for the government for a short time?

MELINDA:
Yes.

INVESTIGATOR *(Looking at the record)*:
Research Assistant for the Bureau of Weights and Measures ... How long did you work there?

MELINDA:
Seven and a half hours.

INVESTIGATOR:
Seven and a half hours! That's not even a full day. Why did you quit?

MELINDA:
I couldn't stand weighing and measuring. Besides there was an attractive man next to me. He had the terrible habit of clicking his pen as he weighed and measured. I couldn't stand the work or his clicking. I knew there was no possibility of a closer relationship. So I left ... *(She goes behind the space panel.)*

INVESTIGATOR *(Clicking his pen unconsciously)*:
I see ... Have you ever had any visitors here?

MELINDA *(From behind the panel)*:
No. You're the first one.

INVESTIGATOR *(Getting up)*:
You've never had any foreign guests?

MELINDA:
I've asked them ... They were too far away ... They couldn't come.

INVESTIGATOR:
Have you ever been convicted of a crime in a state or federal court?

MELINDA *(Appearing from behind the space panel in a large hat with flowers and a long-necked oil can in her hand)*:
Yes ...

INVESTIGATOR:
Yes?

MELINDA *(As they talk, she oils various pieces of equipment.)*:
Parking meter violations. Fifty-one times ...

INVESTIGATOR:

Fifty-one times . . .

MELINDA:

I can't do anything about it. I hate paying money to machines.

INVESTIGATOR:

Do you belong to any international organizations?

MELINDA:

I correspond with some.

INVESTIGATOR:

You're a corresponding member? What organizations?

MELINDA:

No, I simply write to them — scientific organizations, mainly the Federation of International Space Seekers . . .

INVESTIGATOR *(Checking a reference book):*

F 14 . . . Organizations . . . Federation — International — Space — Seekers . . . That's not on the list . . . They publish any books?

MELINDA:

Some technical pamphlets on aspects of space — Physics, Astronomy Mythology . . .

INVESTIGATOR:

Mythology?

MELINDA:

That's when I first became interested in space . . . On top of Moun Olympus, the home of the Greek Gods . . .

INVESTIGATOR:

Greek gods . . .

MELINDA:

When I was in Greece I studied with Dr. Andreas Paxanopolous, the head of the Paxanopolous High Energy Communications Institute . . . He was an unappreciated genius . . .

INVESTIGATOR *(Checking his reference book again):*

Wait a minute, please . . . F 28 . . . Scientists . . . Paxon . . . op-o . . He's not on the list . . . What was he doing?

74

MELINDA:

He discovered an old mythological document. It described Zeus wielding his Awful Thunderbolt to correct wrongs and establish laws ... Dr. Paxanopolous was convinced that the thunderstorms on and around Mount Olympus had special psychological effects ... So together we studied the secrets of thunderstorms in many different places ...

INVESTIGATOR:

Yeah? ... What happened to this Dr. Paxanopolous?

MELINDA:

He died one day in a tragic accident. He fell from an oak tree during a storm ... It was one of the sacred oak trees whose leaves the priests used to interpret the thunderbolt messages from Olympus ... *(She reads a message in Greek reverently and toasts Paxanopolous with her glass.)*

INVESTIGATOR:

I see ... When you came back from Greece you began to build equipment to continue your interest in space ... Would you mind showing me some of your equipment?

MELINDA:

Not at all ... *(She goes behind the panel and comes out in her working cap to lead him to a machine downstage.)*

This is designed to sort out the qualities of space sounds much as you might hear different instruments, different ranges, in the orchestra ... I'll pull the switch for the High Range ... *(She does so and listens. The Investigator strains and can't hear anything.)*

INVESTIGATOR *(Shaking his head)*:

I don't hear anything.

MELINDA *(Explaining)*:

It's too high a frequency for the normal ear to appreciate ...

I've trained myself ... *(Looks at him sceptically.)*

We'll move down a little. I'll try for middle messages ... *(She pulls another switch, looks at him with growing resignation and listens a moment.)*

Too bad ... Nothing in the Middle Ranges ... Down we go, down, nearer to the earth. *(She kneels beside him.)*

The Lower Ranges ... Only two thousand miles above us in space ...
(She pulls another switch.)
Listen! ... *(A low, soft gurgling sound comes out.)*

INVESTIGATOR *(Smiling suddenly):*

Hey, somebody ordered a cab! *(Melinda bangs on the piece of equipment.)*
I hear something now ... *(The sound stops abruptly.)*
It's gone!

MELINDA *(Explaining):*

The messages of space are very brief ... You must train yourself to catch them quickly as the eye catches the swoop of a bird. *(She leads him over to another panel with some handles and levers.)*

INVESTIGATOR *(Cautiously, but more and more interested):*
What does this machine do?

MELINDA:

It sends up flights of tiny electronic ears to record space messages ... They fly through the air like arrows of light at twice the speed of sound ... Then they hover in space ...

INVESTIGATOR *(Trying to calculate on his fingers):*
Twice the speed of sound ...

MELINDA:

If you don't mind helping me, it's easier to operate with four hands than two.

INVESTIGATOR:

I'll be glad to help.

MELINDA *(Gives him some heavy earphones to put on. The earphones tend to deafen him so she shouts her instructions louder and louder):* Just hold this lever *(she points)* with both hands ...
I'll count to three and pull ...

INVESTIGATOR:

Pull? ... Right *(He gives her a thumbs up signal and bends tensely to his duty)*

MELINDA *(Loudly):*
I'll be on these switches over here. *(She crosses to the panel.)*
Ready?

INVESTIGATOR:
Ready ...

MELINDA:
1 - 2 - 3 - PULL! *(He pulls on the count of two and the lever comes out. He walks over and holds it up apologetically to Melinda just as she is about to command, "Pull!")*

MELINDA:
I'm sorry ... It doesn't seem to work today ... Short circuit in the wiring some place probably ... You can see why it's only the equipment of a fan ...

INVESTIGATOR:
A what?

MELINDA:
A space fan ...

INVESTIGATOR:
A space fan?

MELINDA:
That's right.

INVESTIGATOR *(Laughing with relief):*
That puts a different light on things.

MELINDA:
What kind of light?

INVESTIGATOR *(Smiling):*
You know, they thought possibly ...

MELINDA:
They thought I was subversive ...

INVESTIGATOR *(Protesting and justifying them):*
No, but they can't afford to take chances when it's a matter of security. A fan may be eccentric, but he's normal. A fan is perfectly all right.

MELINDA:

Are you calling me eccentric?

INVESTIGATOR:

Of course not. I'm a fan like you. A baseball fan.

MELINDA:

I suppose there is a distant similarity. But some fans have more ambition, more endurance. The quality of endurance is often the test of the real fan.

INVESTIGATOR:

Have you ever sat through a twenty-six inning game on an empty stomach? That takes quite a bit of endurance from the crowd. But they're always friendly.

MELINDA:

A crowd may be composed of fans, but it's not the same thing. The real fan learns to be alone. He has a passion to follow. When the crowd moves in, the pleasure goes out.

INVESTIGATOR *(Dubiously)*:

I don't know. It's more fun, sharing.

MELINDA:

More fun, private.

INVESTIGATOR:

More fun, sharing.

MELINDA *(Making a game out of it, insisting)*:

More fun, *private*.

INVESTIGATOR:

Sharing.

MELINDA:

Private.

INVESTIGATOR *(Doggedly)*:

Sharing.

MELINDA *(Taunting him)*:

Private. You're a socialist!

INVESTIGATOR *(Turning away indignantly):* I hate socialism! Before I go, I'd like to ask you one more question . . .

MELINDA:
Aren't you a fan of anything besides baseball?

INVESTIGATOR:
Well . . .

MELINDA:
What is it?

INVESTIGATOR:
The Civil War.

MELINDA *(With delight):*
You're a history fan!

INVESTIGATOR *(Cautiously):*
I'm just a beginner really. I haven't told them at the office.

MELINDA:
Why not?

INVESTIGATOR *(Uncomfortably):*
They don't like us to have too much of an aesthetic interest.

MELINDA *(Still delighted with the discovery of his fanship):*
You belong to all those Civil War Book Clubs?

INVESTIGATOR:
Well, a few . . .

MELINDA:
And you visit the battlefields!

INVESTIGATOR *(Confessing):*
Sometimes . . . In summer vacations . . .

MELINDA *(Pressing him):*
Every summer?

INVESTIGATOR:
When I can persuade my wife . . .

MELINDA:
Your wife?

INVESTIGATOR *(Bitterly)*:
She doesn't like the Civil War.

MELINDA *(Sympathetically)*:
That's too bad.

INVESTIGATOR:
She says the Civil War is out of date. What's that got to do with the facts of it?

MELINDA:
Nothing.

INVESTIGATOR *(Confessing indignantly)*:
Last night she said the Civil War was boring. She won't go there again this summer. It's too hot in those places for her. She sweats. She can't sleep. She complains about the insects . . .

MELINDA:
Heat and insects are small deterrents for a real fan.

INVESTIGATOR *(Bitterly)*:
I've tried to make her one. I've taken her to Shiloh and Gettysburg and Chancelorsville and Bull Run . . . I showed her the hills of concealment . . . I showed her how they attacked down the slopes . . I showed her the traps in the valleys . . . I even showed her the bugle that sounded General Lee's last attack!

MELINDA:
I'm sorry.

INVESTIGATOR *(Pulling himself back to the task at hand)*:
Well, I'd like to ask you one more question . . .

MELINDA:
Would you rather have Robert E. Lee or Dwight Eisenhower for a general?

INVESTIGATOR *(Protesting)*:
You can't compare the two. Lee was a cavalry general, not an administrator. Now you take a modern war, it's all over the world. You got all kinds of countries, languages and weapons to deal with. So you need an administrator like Eisenhower. But Lee, he was a real tactician in the field. He didn't need memoranda and forms and files and . . .

80

MELINDA:
I can see you prefer the past ...

INVESTIGATOR:
Who said I prefer the past? I'm perfectly content with the present.

MELINDA:
Perfectly?

INVESTIGATOR:
There is no such thing as perfectly!

MELINDA:
There is in space, in the infinity of it.

INVESTIGATOR:
Infinity is too much.

MELINDA:
Earth is too little.

INVESTIGATOR:
Isn't that escaping?

MELINDA:
If there is a trap, one has the right to escape.

INVESTIGATOR:
I guess so ... Now about my question ...

MELINDA:
What are we spending all that money for to reach the moon?

INVESTIGATOR:
Scientific research, of course. Please ...

MELINDA:
We'll never get to the moon as long as your engineers and mathematicians continue to be so careless.

INVESTIGATOR *(Protesting):*
They aren't careless. They're very responsible people ...

MELINDA:
Why did they leave a hyphen out of the mathematics on that last Venus shot?

INVESTIGATOR *(Bewildered)*:
  Hyphen?

MELINDA *(Pointing)*:
  Some careless mathematician left a hyphen out of the computer's instructions. This caused it to transmit incorrect steering signals to the spacecraft ...

INVESTIGATOR *(Dazed)*:
  You mean a hyphen ...

MELINDA *(She pushes him downstage into the position of the computer and she becomes the spacecraft as she illustrates)*:
  When ground control loses radio contact with a spacecraft antenna, that's an emergency! The antenna is very sensitive! *(Imitating the spacecraft antenna, she begins to demonstrate with her hands and arms.)*
  Immediately, the antenna begins to maneuver the spacecraft in an up-and-down "searching" movement. Search! Search, until contact is re-established ...

INVESTIGATOR *(Impressed)*:
  That's amazing.

MELINDA *(Excited, continuing)*:
  Automatic radio signals are sent out from the spacecraft. They tell the computer on the ground that this veering, this up and down searching movement, is taking place. The hyphen is then fed carefully into the computer and tells the spacecraft not to worry.

INVESTIGATOR *(Fascinated)*:
  You mean a hyphen says don't worry?

MELINDA:
  Exactly. The omission of the hyphen caused the space craft to send out a series of frenzied signals ...

INVESTIGATOR *(Crying out)*:
  What was it signaling?

MELINDA *(Crossing with frenzied signals)*:
  Find me! Find me! Correct my course!

INVESTIGATOR *(Following, intrigued)*:
Marvelous!

MELINDA *(Sadly, seeing the spacecraft lost above)*:
But it was no use. The spacecraft was lost.

INVESTIGATOR *(Dazed, echoing her mood, staring up at the destruction)*:
Because of a hyphen...

MELINDA *(Vehemently)*:
Yes, because of carelessness in leaving out a hyphen, eighteen and a half million dollars of spacecraft bound for Venus was blown up in the air.

INVESTIGATOR *(Muttering)*:
Computers are murder.

MELINDA:
You can't blame the computers. It's the people who feed 'em. A computer must be fed properly, with the proper diet of language, a language never before published in books. Even today, these languages are available only in out of the way places.

INVESTIGATOR:
What places?

MELINDA:
Mimeographed places, handwritten places... I wrote to people... Many of them answered. They sent me all sorts of scribbled things ... And I scribbled things back to them. Then I began to build my own equipment...

INVESTIGATOR *(Suddenly remembering his duty as an investigator)*:
Well, you'll have to be careful about interference... But I'm sure everything will be all right if you just give me your papers... Then I can explain about your being a space fan...

MELINDA *(Staring at him)*:
You want my papers...

INVESTIGATOR:
It's the easiest way to convince them...

MELINDA:

I don't have any papers.

INVESTIGATOR:

I mean the scribbled things you mentioned.

MELINDA:

They're only fragments, jottings on backs of envelopes, menus, programs, any odd piece of paper to hand. Most of them aren't even scientific. You couldn't read the handwriting.

INVESTIGATOR:

We've got special people for that.

MELINDA:

I don't have many left. I throw them away. I don't like a clutter.

INVESTIGATOR:

I'll just take what you have. That will satisfy them.

MELINDA:

Why should I satisfy them? I give you my word. The scribblings are unimportant.

INVESTIGATOR:

I'm sorry . . . I can't take anybody's word.

MELINDA:

You can never trust anyone?

INVESTIGATOR:

That would be the end of the investigations.

MELINDA:

Never?

INVESTIGATOR:

Never.

MELINDA:

Never is terribly severe.

INVESTIGATOR *(Defensively)*:

Maybe a little at first . . . You get used to it . . . You'd be surprised at how much people tell you is incorrect.

84

MELINDA:
  False or incorrect?

INVESTIGATOR:
  What's the difference?

MELINDA:
  False is a lie; incorrect can be a trick of the imagination, don't you think?

INVESTIGATOR:
  It all comes to the same thing — wrong information.

MELINDA *(Bitterly)*:
  I would hate to live in your world of wrong information. *(She looks at him with scorn and goes off behind the space panel. The Investigator, trying again to fulfill the demands of his job, begins to snoop around the panel as he talks. He pulls out some of the roll of tape, tries to stuff it under his coat, and discovers this is impossible.)*

INVESTIGATOR:
  That's what they taught us to do in our training program. It was full of wrong information. Every teacher had a different method of giving us wrong information. We had to find out the facts.

MELINDA *(Ironically, from behind the panel)*:
  They must have been excellent teachers.

INVESTIGATOR *(As he speaks, he pulls out the tape. Melinda appears in a mask above the space panel, looking down at him. He turns away and opens his briefcase, intending to put the tape in it. Behind his back, she pulls the tape back through the panel. He turns around just in time to see the tape disappearing as she reels it in. He jumps for the end of the tape, but it's gone. He turns back and fumbles with the briefcase on his knees.)*:
  I hated them ... My wife made me take the course ... She wanted me to get a white collar job ... The teachers were always trying to trap us ... One gave the same lecture over and over again ... It sounded true, but it was always a little wrong ... Then he'd test us to see if we caught the error ... He'd say: "If you want to be an investigator, you have to find the one clear, dry place in a sea of mud."

(Melinda, in the mask of the Witch Queen of Space, pounces in on him):

MELINDA *(Mocking him as she darts around him):*
I'm the Witch Queen of Space!... I jam your radio transmission...
I hover over your satellites...

INVESTIGATOR *(He steps toward her.):*
Come on, this is no time...

MELINDA *(Zooming away from him):*
I fly away from you on my space scooter... The Northern Lights
shine between us... I dazzle your eyes with shooting stars...

INVESTIGATOR *(Impatiently):*
Don't fool around. I need those papers...

MELINDA:
High up in the Milky Way I build my palace out of Moonshine...

INVESTIGATOR:
Stop it, please...

MELINDA:
I use my Cosmic Ray vision... The Earthmen disintegrate in their
lies...

INVESTIGATOR *(Pleading):*
I never lied to you! This is my first case. Please, where'd you hide
the papers...

MELINDA:
Look! Where's your space vision? *(She points to the back of the
stage.)*
The papers are hidden on Planet X...

INVESTIGATOR *(Going in that direction):*
You mean back there?

MELINDA *(Mockingly, drawing him downstage):*
Gone!... Someone has moved them to sanctuary... Look for them
in the third orbit...*(She points at a drawer.)*

86

INVESTIGATOR *(Moving)*:

You mean in that drawer? *(He goes to the drawer and opens it. Nothing.)*

MELINDA:

Empty!... Stolen by the Witch Queen of Space! *(She holds up a box high above her head.)*

INVESTIGATOR:

Are they in that box?... Please give them to me... I'll see that you're cleared... I'll tell them that you're all right...

MELINDA *(Jumping on a table and holding the box high above her head.)*
The Witch Queen of Space holds high the Treasure Chest!

INVESTIGATOR:

Give it to me!

MELINDA:

The Witch Queen swoops down *(she swoops down)* and surrenders the Treasure Chest... *(She jams the box into his stomach and he recoils.)*

INVESTIGATOR:

Thanks... I'm sorry...

MELINDA *(Keeping after him)*:

Fly! Fly away before she claws you!

INVESTIGATOR *(Retreating)*:

I won't forget this...

MELINDA:

Fly!

INVESTIGATOR *(Getting his hat and briefcase)*:

I'll tell them you're only a space fan...

MELINDA:

Fly, Master Thief!

INVESTIGATOR *(As he goes off, pursued by her)*:

They won't bother you again...

MELINDA:

Fly! *(She chases him off. He hurries out uncomfortably, clutching the box as though it hurts him physically. Melinda stares after him for a long moment. Then she takes off her mask. Her loneliness is apparent. She turns on several switches and moves slowly toward the space panel. The high, eerie music of space is heard.)*

MELINDA *(Taking up the microphone at the space panel, she begins to speak. Her soliloquy builds to a high, fantastic intensity.)*

Come in, Commander ... You read me ... All systems Go! ... Blast off! ... Soar space craft! ... Roar like the Saturn rocket for the moon ... Throw out all the earthbound equipment ... You can't come home again ... Float in that weightlessness ... Light as a feather in the winds ... Dead center on course ... Accelerating over Africa ... Approaching Greece ... Come in, Paxanopolous, come in ... Messages sing over your grave ... You taught me about the gods ... This investigator was your Master Thief, your God of Commerce and the Market ... He was your Guide of the Dead ... Why did you send him? ... To bring me to you? ... He's gone now ... We're free ... Rendezvous point coming up ... Space ships moving together for final voyage ... Equipment working perfectly ... Slow trajectory of approach ... Nearer, nearer ... Touching ... Not even a bump ... So gentle ... Here we are, Paxanopolous alone in space ... I hear your messages at last ... I hear them sing Do you hear mine? ... I send you the music of space! *(She listens raptly to the high, eerie sounds and music of space. The Investigator has returned at the end of her speech and is also listening He is angry and tense because he has discovered that the box is empty. His suspicions grow as he hears the equipment working Finally, he breaks in.)*

INVESTIGATOR *(He rushes to the space panel and takes the microphone away from her.):*

You tricked me! *(A garbled, protesting Chinese voice is heard and the Investigator says)* That's all right, Mr. Wong. I think we've found the trouble. *(He speaks tensely into the microphone.)*

If anyone is listening, ignore messages from the home of Melinda Davis, 4269 Mira Loma Street! *(He hangs up the microphone and rushes around among the equipment, turning off switches hap-*

hazardly, and shouting his accusations at Melinda.) Do you realize what you've done? You were responsible for the complaints about interference ... You've been interfering with the lives of other people! Do you know what's happened? ... A Chinese restaurant with radio dispatched delivery service sent twenty-seven orders of Moo Goo Gai Pan to an empty parking lot! ... Tickets to the Church Bazaar were delivered to the football stadium! Truckloads of newspapers ended up in a mortuary! ... And that's only local interference ... Who knows what you've done to the international situation? ... And you know damn well there aren't any papers in this box!

(He slams the box down.)

Now I want your papers! ... Give me your papers! ... Where are they?

MELINDA *(Staring at him calmly):*

I'm glad you came back ... You're just in time for the burning.

INVESTIGATOR:

What burning?

MELINDA *(She disappears behind the space panel.):*

I'm going to burn all my papers.

INVESTIGATOR *(Following her around):*

You can't do that! It's against the law to burn evidence!

You'll never get away with it! *(She reappears again with a large incinerator.)*

What are you going to do with that?

MELINDA:

My burning machine ... You can be a witness ...

INVESTIGATOR:

I can't be a witness! ... It's my duty to stop you ...

MELINDA *(Proceeding):*

Stop me then. *(He takes up the incinerator, cradling it protectively in his arms. She takes it away from him and puts it down firmly.)* All you have to do is watch ...

INVESTIGATOR:

I can't watch ... I've never watched before ...

89

MELINDA:

Turn your face away ... You won't see the beginning ...

INVESTIGATOR *(He turns his face away and begins to plead again.)*
Look, you know it isn't my fault ... I didn't want this job ... Give
me the papers ... *(She doesn't answer, as she gathers some tattered
papers for burning.)* It's not safe to burn here ... There are fire
laws! ...
Please don't burn those papers ...

MELINDA *(She begins to burn her tattered scribblings.):*
Poor scribblings, preparations, fragments, there's never any comple-
tion for you ... I jot you down as numbers, equations ... I line you
up as perfect forms, but there are no perfect forms ...Only changing forms ... *(She reads a scribbling.)*
Notes for a London conference: "The tea is lukewarm."
*(She lights it with a match and throws it into the incinerator. The
lights go down into an increasingly red glow for the burning scene.
She picks up an old cardboard menu and reads)*
Scribbled on the back of a Parisian menu: "What is the power of
thrust necessary for escape?"

INVESTIGATOR:

Escape?

MELINDA *(Continuing with the burning ritual):*
Burn, symbols! Fly into space! Burn into ashes! Cremate, consume,
destroy! *(She goes behind the panel and comes back with more
papers.)* Notes from Russia ...

INVESTIGATOR:

No!

MELINDA:

Tsarist Russia! Pushkin's vision of the future. *(She laughs bitterly
and drops the papers into the incinerator. She picks up an old
envelope.)* On a Roman envelope: "Visited the Keats museum ...
What a small space to die in" ... Burn the past! Let the future
of space glow in the flames! ... *(She rushes across the stage to
pick up another pile of scribblings.)* Asia, too, postcard of a Japa-
nese Zen temple ... *(She reads the postcard.)* "What is the sound
of one hand clapping?" Burn! *(She throws the postcard in.)* The

sound of silence, eternal space ... *(She turns to the Investigator.)* How can you report unless you participate? ... Do you want to be nothing except an investigator?

INVESTIGATOR *(Uneasily)*:
Don't be silly ... You can't fool me again ...

MELINDA:
Can't you see? There won't be any more interference from the equipment.

INVESTIGATOR:
I told you I can't take your word.

MELINDA:
You don't have to ... Help me burn ... Then we'll take care of the equipment.

INVESTIGATOR:
OK ... *(She leads him over to the incinerator and gives him some papers.)*

MELINDA:
You know they're of no value now ... Travel notes, musings, old formulas ...

INVESTIGATOR *(Slowly)*:
Yeah, there's nothing here ... *(He reads a scribbling on a postcard.)* "How do you like this view of Rio De Janeiro? ... The sand is so white ... If it were only possible to travel forever" ... *(He drops it in automatically and stares at it.)*

MELINDA:
You see? Long live travel!

INVESTIGATOR *(Automatically)*:
Long live travel ...

MELINDA:
Long live travel to the Civil War sites! *(She throws in some papers and they both circle around the incinerator slowly.)*

INVESTIGATOR *(Getting into the spirit)*:
Long live travel to Gettysburg! *(He throws in a scribbling.)* Long

live Shiloh! *(He throws in another scribbling.)* Long live Bull Run
(Another scribbling goes in.)

MELINDA *(Laughing as she reads an old postcard):*
Postcard from Paris ... "Dear Mother: Why are you such a Puritan
I can't even enjoy Paris?" *(She throws it in.)*

INVESTIGATOR *(Laughing with her as he reads an old letter):*
How about this one?... "As a girl I was always better with facts
than boys" ... *(They laugh as he drops it in, she cries out)*

MELINDA:
Puritan mothers!

INVESTIGATOR:
The family is dead!

MELINDA:
Burn the past!

INVESTIGATOR:
Burn the past! *(Melinda rushes over, gets her large handbag, and
cries out)*

MELINDA:
Burn the present! *(She begins to rummage in the handbag.)*

INVESTIGATOR *(Staring at her):*
Burn the present?

MELINDA *(Pulling some papers out of the handbag):*
Charge accounts ... Last letters from stupid relatives ... *(She throws
them in.)*

INVESTIGATOR *(Impulsively he reaches for his wallet and begins to take
out various items.):*
Detergent housewives who hate the Civil War! *(He throws in a photo
of his wife.)*

MELINDA:
Bank stubs ... savings book ... *(She throws them in, as the burning
ritual builds in intensity.)*

INVESTIGATOR:
Identification card with finger prints and photo! *(He throws it in.)*

LINDA *(Laughing)*:
It wasn't a very good likeness anyway! ... Life insurance policy ...
  Guaranteed payment after death ... *(She drops it in and they circle
  gayly around the incinerator.)*

INVESTIGATOR:
Social Security ... *(He drops it in.)*

LINDA:
Hospital safety plan ... *(She drops it in.)*

INVESTIGATOR:
Civil Service ... *(He drops it in.)*

LINDA:
Charity donations ... *(She throws them in.)*

INVESTIGATOR:
Investigator Club membership ... *(He throws it in.)*

LINDA:
Parking meter violations ... *(She throws them in.)*

INVESTIGATOR *(Caught up in the frenzy, he throws in his wallet.)*
Burn!

LINDA *(Emptying the rest of the contents of her handbag)*:
Burn!

INVESTIGATOR *(Tearing off his coat compulsively and stuffing it in)*:
Burn!

LINDA *(Stuffing in her handbag)*:
Escape!

INVESTIGATOR *(Echoing her)*:
Escape! *(Panting, they stare at the flames in the incinerator.)*

LINDA *(Looking at her empty hands)*:
They're all gone. I'm sorry ... There aren't any more ...

INVESTIGATOR *(Dully, still echoing her)*:
Gone ...

LINDA:
Would it help if I promise to save them again for next time?

INVESTIGATOR *(Pulling himself together)*:
  There won't be a next time.

MELINDA:
  There are only next times. I hope they won't make it too difficult f
  you.

INVESTIGATOR *(Mechanically)*:
  I hope they won't make it too difficult for *you*.

MELINDA:
  Perhaps I can help. I can show you something that might make
  easier for you.

INVESTIGATOR:
  It doesn't matter.

MELINDA *(Almost timidly)*:
  I'd like to show it to you. All you have to do is put it on.

INVESTIGATOR:
  Put what on?

MELINDA *(She goes behind the space panel and brings out a helmet.*
  A helmet.

INVESTIGATOR:
  What helmet?

MELINDA:
  A space helmet.

INVESTIGATOR *(Backing away)*:
  Where'd you get that?

MELINDA:
  It's mine. One day I would like to give it a real test. Try it on.

INVESTIGATOR:
  I don't think I'd better.

MELINDA:
  I'll put mine on. We can tune in to each other.

INVESTIGATOR:
  No thanks. It won't be necessary.

ELINDA:

You were making such progress in your investigation. Your report will be incomplete.

VESTIGATOR *(Reluctantly):*

All right. I'll do it. For the report.

ELINDA:

For your real work, your real play, for the sacredness of investigation. Relax now ... You'll receive messages through space ... Through the clarity of space ... Weightless messages ... A new clarity and lightness of language ... Polished and pure ... Beyond people ... Beyond confused emotions ... Beyond the force of brutal gravity ... You'll hear the peace of space ...

(A woman's voice is heard singing offstage):

> *"The shapes our searching arms*
> *make in the empty air*
> *are women's bodies*
> *that when the wind and rain*
> *possess our sight*
> *we have that grace to touch,*
> *those white shapes to know,*
> *and keep a sanity*
> *for love."*

(Slowly, the lights are lowered. From here to the end of the play, the mood is a measured, poignant dance to the high woodwind or electronic music. The two voices are heard only on tape. The effect is of communication over a tremendous distance, of a strange, inevitable separation, although they are really very close together.)

ELINDA:

Can you hear me, Mr. Investigator? Can you hear me?

VESTIGATOR:

I hear you perfectly.

ELINDA:

Perfectly?

VESTIGATOR:

Perfectly ... Funny, I've never used that word before.

95

MELINDA:

Watch out. You'll become a space fan, too.

INVESTIGATOR:

I feel as if I'm floating.

MELINDA:

Higher . . . Higher . . . You are floating . . . In weightlessness . . .

INVESTIGATOR:

Floating . . .

MELINDA:

Lie down . . . *(He lies down.)*

Move your arms and legs . . . *(He does so.)*

Raise your feet in the air . . . *(He raises his feet in his ordinary brown street shoes.)*

Your heavy flying boots weigh nothing . . . How does that feel?

INVESTIGATOR:

Wonderful. No effort at all.

MELINDA:

Your life is not just vertical any more. It's horizontal.

INVESTIGATOR:

Horizontal is marvelous.

MELINDA:

Do you feel the difference? Vertical is a rigid skyscraper.

INVESTIGATOR:

Horizontal is a cloud of comfort.

MELINDA:

Now you're beginning your space metaphors.

INVESTIGATOR:

Horizontal is beyond heaven.

MELINDA:

Good . . .

INVESTIGATOR:

Horizontal is the endless glitter of stars, infinite horizons . . .

Yvonne McElroy and Charles Cioffi in Edward Call's production of *The Space Fan* at the Tyrone Guthrie Theatre in Minneapolis.

MELINDA:

Again!

INVESTIGATOR:

Horizontal is the moon of your eyes.

MELINDA *(Gayly)*:

Again!

INVESTIGATOR:

I love space. I love the moon of your eyes. I love you horizontally.

MELINDA:

Try to lift your arms. *(He stands up and stretches his arms up.)*
Higher ... Higher ... What are you reaching for?

INVESTIGATOR:

A world invisible, star beyond star.

MELINDA:

Are there any people there?

INVESTIGATOR:

I don't see any.

MELINDA:

Can you feel any?

INVESTIGATOR:

Nothing but stars, cold stars, burning stars.

MELINDA:

Time is space, eternal distance.

INVESTIGATOR:

It's like a dance. I never danced before.

MELINDA:

Neither did I.

INVESTIGATOR:

Will you dance with me? *(High woodwinds, flutes and oboes, or high
eerie electronic sounds until the end of the play. They dance a short,
formal, poignant dance of a meeting that is separation, and a separation that is meeting.)*

MELINDA:

Do you hear music?

INVESTIGATOR:

Is that what it's called?

MELINDA:

The music of space.

INVESTIGATOR:

I never heard such melodies before.

MELINDA:

Look out. Look down. Look up. *(He does so.)*
What do you see?

INVESTIGATOR:

Distance. Eternal distance.

MELINDA:

Look at your watch.

INVESTIGATOR:

It's stopped.

MELINDA:

What time is it?

INVESTIGATOR:

No time. Time has stopped.

MELINDA:

Time is space.

INVESTIGATOR:

I can see God now.

MELINDA:

What does he look like?

INVESTIGATOR:

God is space. *(Silence. The music continues, very high, very distant.)*
For the first time in my life, I feel that I've become a real investigator.

MELINDA:
  You *are* an Investigator.

INVESTIGATOR *(Exultantly)*:
  You're a Space Fan. *(Then whispering)* I love you . . .

MELINDA *(Whispering)*:
  I love you in space.

INVESTIGATOR:
  Will you dance with me again, my love?

MELINDA:
  Yes, my darling. *(They begin to dance slowly, gravely. The lights dim further.)*

INVESTIGATOR:
  If we could only *never* return to earth . . .

MELINDA:
  That may be possible some day . . .
  (They continue to dance. As they dance, the woman's voice is heard offstage singing):

> *"The shapes our searching arms*
> *make in the empty air*
> *are women's bodies*
> *that when the wind and rain*
> *possess our sight*
> *we have that grace to touch,*
> *those white shapes to know,*
> *and keep a sanity for love."*

(The lights dim slowly to black out and the play ends.)

INTERMISSION

99

THE MASTER:

A Play of Commitment

*(As the lights come up slowly, percussion music is heard played by the
Assistant, dressed in a black sweater and pants, who sits on a stand at
the rear of the stage. A woman's voice is heard singing:*

*The shapes our searching arms
make in the empty air
are women's bodies
that when the wind and rain
possess our sight
we have that grace to touch,
those white shapes to know,
and keep a sanity
for love.*

100

The Master and the Candidate enter, cross the stage to the beat of per-cussion music, bow to each other, and then bow to the audience.)

THE MASTER *(Smoking a cigar)*:
  I am the Master.

THE CANDIDATE:
  I am the Candidate.

(The Master is dressed in a white robe, the Candidate in a red, white, and blue robe. The Master is a heavy set, imposing man, while the Candidate is an attractive young woman, aggressive, yet roman-tically naive. After the introductions, she sits on a chair at the front of the stage, waiting and preening herself nervously for the examination. The Master goes to his table and chair upstage at stage right. He signals the Assistant who brings a tray of cigars and cigarettes which the Master arranges carefully on the table. Finally, the Master gestures. A bell is rung by the Assistant and the Candidate moves toward the table. The Master motions to her to be seated. He begins to question her, checking her record sheet before him casually, feeling her out.)

THE MASTER:
  Name?

THE CANDIDATE:
  Diana Johnson.

THE MASTER:
  Last name first, please.

THE CANDIDATE:
  Johnson, Diana.

THE MASTER:
  Rank?

THE CANDIDATE:
  Candidate.

THE MASTER:
  For the degree of mastery. Specific or general?

THE CANDIDATE:
  General.

THE MASTER:
Including Religion, Physical Education, Science, War, and the Humanities?

THE CANDIDATE:
Yes, Sir.

THE MASTER:
Your Candidate number, please.

THE CANDIDATE:
452691.

THE MASTER:
Good. Do you smoke?

THE CANDIDATE:
Please.

THE MASTER *(Unrolling a sign with a vivid illustration and the warning "Smoking Causes Cancer!")*:
Help yourself. *(He watches her closely as she selects a cigarette. He lights it for her.)*

THE MASTER:
How many cigarettes do you smoke a day?

THE CANDIDATE:
It's hard to say. Half a pack maybe. More if I'm studying.

THE MASTER:
It isn't safe. Don't you believe in Statistics?

THE CANDIDATE:
It depends on the Statistics.

THE MASTER:
What Statistics?

THE CANDIDATE *(Cautiously)*:
It depends on the relationship.

THE MASTER:
On what relationship?

THE CANDIDATE:
What the statistics relate to. Objects or subjects.

THE MASTER:
You believe in the Statistics of Subjects?

THE CANDIDATE:
Only objects can be measured.

THE MASTER *(Getting up):*
Isn't a cigarette an object?

THE CANDIDATE:
Yes, but the person smoking is a subject. Pleasure can ignore danger.

THE MASTER:
You smoke for pleasure to ignore danger?

THE CANDIDATE:
Sometimes. Mainly I smoke because other people smoke.

THE MASTER *(Crossing to her):*
You are smoking because I am smoking?

THE CANDIDATE:
Yes, sir.

THE MASTER:
Exchange smokes. *(He gives her his cigar and takes her cigarette.)*
You are smoking because I am smoking?

THE CANDIDATE:
Yes, sir.

THE MASTER:
Is the pleasure greater or lesser?

THE CANDIDATE:
Lesser.

THE MASTER:
Why? Because of the cigar?

THE CANDIDATE:
No, sir. Because I merely smoke to keep other people company.

THE MASTER:
   You are a conformist?

THE CANDIDATE:
   Yes, much of the time.

THE MASTER:
   You think it's always bad to be a conformist?

THE CANDIDATE *(Cautiously):*
   Sometimes.

THE MASTER:
   It is bad to be obedient to parents?

THE CANDIDATE:
   No.

THE MASTER:
   If you are always obedient to parents, you are a conformist?

THE CANDIDATE:
   No ... Yes ...

THE MASTER:
   It is bad to be a conformist?

THE CANDIDATE:
   Yes and no.

THE MASTER:
   How much yes and how much no?

THE CANDIDATE:
   Half and half.

THE MASTER:
   Instant?

THE CANDIDATE:
   No, slow. The right balance ... It is hard to tell ...

THE MASTER:
   Do you believe in Instant Conformity?

THE CANDIDATE:
   Yes and no.

THE MASTER *(Ordering)*:
Lie down on your back ... I said lie down on your back!

THE CANDIDATE *(Getting up)*:
Yes ... *(Changing her mind)* and no ...

THE MASTER:
You won't obey my order?

THE CANDIDATE *(Unsure)*:
Is it an order or a question?

THE MASTER *(Ordering, and leaving no doubt by the tone of his voice that it is an order)*:
Lie down on your back! *(The Candidate lies down on her back.)*
You are a conformist.

THE CANDIDATE:
I obey orders.

THE MASTER:
Lift your feet in the air. *(She does so.)*

THE MASTER:
Do the bicycle ... Higher ... Faster. *(She begins to do the bicycle exercise.)*
Circulation is good for the brain.
Enough. Stop exercising. You are a conformist.

THE CANDIDATE *(Panting a little, she stops.)*:
I obey orders.

THE MASTER:
Spit on the floor. *(She does so.)*   Wipe it up.

THE CANDIDATE:
How?

THE MASTER:
Use your hand. *(Slowly, she does so.)* You are an Instant Conformist.

THE CANDIDATE *(Bitterly)*:
I obey orders.

THE MASTER:
You hate me?

THE CANDIDATE:
Yes and no.

THE MASTER:
Kiss me. *(Slowly, she goes to him and gives him a short kiss.)*

THE CANDIDATE:
The kiss of obedience. I obey orders.

THE MASTER:
Kiss me again. *(She gives him a short, fierce kiss as he blows a puff of cigar smoke in her face.)* Describe the kiss.

THE CANDIDATE:
The kiss of hate.

THE MASTER:
Is that what you think of a kiss? What is a kiss?

THE CANDIDATE:
The highest gift of love.

THE MASTER:
Then hate is never part of love?

THE CANDIDATE:
Yes and no.

THE MASTER:
Give me the kiss of love. *(She gives him a passionate kiss.)* Describe the kiss.

THE CANDIDATE:
The kiss of love.

THE MASTER:
Then love can be a greater affirmation?

THE CANDIDATE:
Yes and no.

THE MASTER:
Yes and no is a cliché.

THE CANDIDATE:
Yes.

THE MASTER:
Every cliché is bad.

THE CANDIDATE:
No.

THE MASTER:
Yes and no is an equivocation. American power does not permit equivocation.

THE CANDIDATE:
Yes, Sir.

THE MASTER:
American power says Yes.

THE CANDIDATE *(Softly):*
Yes.

THE MASTER:
A loud, affirmative *Yes!*

THE CANDIDATE:
Yes.

THE MASTER:
In an optimistic, smiling tone!

THE CANDIDATE *(In an optimistic, smiling tone).*
Yes!

THE MASTER:
Not just once, but several times.

THE CANDIDATE:
Yes! Yes! Yes! Yes! Yes!

THE MASTER:
Even in the midst of tragedy...

THE CANDIDATE:
Yes!

THE MASTER:
...in an optimistic, smiling tone...

107

THE CANDIDATE:
Yes!

THE MASTER:
Yes and no are Un-American.

THE CANDIDATE:
Yes.

THE MASTER:
Yes and No are Zen Buddhism.

THE CANDIDATE:
Yes.

THE MASTER:
Screw Zen Buddhism!

THE CANDIDATE:
Yes.

THE MASTER:
The West belongs to Jesus Christ.

THE CANDIDATE:
Yes.

THE MASTER:
And to the President of the United States.

THE CANDIDATE:
Yes.

THE MASTER:
And, above all, to the Constitution of the United States.

THE CANDIDATE:
Yes.

THE MASTER:
No is Un-Constitutional.

THE CANDIDATE:
Yes.

THE MASTER:
You will never again say No.

HE CANDIDATE:
No ... *Yes.*

HE MASTER *(The Assistant brings a container of coffee with a lid on it and takes the lid off carefully.)* :
Take a coffee break. *(The tempo, which has built up rapidly, slows suddenly.)*

HE CANDIDATE *(Accepting the coffee)* :
Thank you, Master.

HE MASTER:
Peace is perfect.

HE CANDIDATE *(Echoing him)* :
Peace is perfect.

HE MASTER:
Take a sip. *(She does so.)*
Pass it to me. *(She gives it to him. He takes a sip.)*
Peace is perfect. *(He hands it back to her. She takes a sip.)*

HE CANDIDATE:
Peace is perfect.

HE MASTER:
Peace passeth all understanding.

HE CANDIDATE:
Yes.

HE MASTER *(Pushing her on)* :
Peace is beyond all reason.

HE CANDIDATE:
Yes.

HE MASTER:
Take another sip. *(She takes a sip.)*
Hand it to me. *(She hands it to him. He takes a sip.)*
We are at peace. Blessed be the peaecmakers.

HE CANDIDATE:
Blessed be the peacemakers.

THE MASTER *(Rising and reflecting)*:
   But peace is a difficult word.

THE CANDIDATE:
   Yes.

THE MASTER:
   Put on the uniform. *(The Candidate takes off her robe and puts on the officer's jacket.)*

THE MASTER:
   What rank are you?

THE CANDIDATE:
   Second Lieutenant.

THE MASTER:
   Shavetail, you call it.

THE CANDIDATE:
   Shavetail.

THE MASTER:
   What are the three great principles of an officer throughout history?

THE CANDIDATE:
   Courage, nobility, generosity.

THE MASTER:
   In American terms?

THE CANDIDATE:
   Guts, brass, hand-outs.

THE MASTER *(Showing her a swagger-stick)*:
   I give you a symbol of brass. What is it called?

THE CANDIDATE:
   Swagger stick.

THE MASTER *(Offering it to her)*:
   Accept it.

THE CANDIDATE:
   I can't accept it.

110

HE MASTER:
Why not?

HE CANDIDATE:
I'm only a second lieutenant. The swagger stick is an optional item of interference.

HE MASTER:
According to whom?

HE CANDIDATE:
The Commandant of the Marines. He says, "If you feel the need of it, carry it."

HE MASTER *(Commanding):*
Feel the need of it!

HE CANDIDATE *(Reaching for it slowly):*
Yes, Sir.

HE MASTER:
Swagger with it. *(She handles it as if it were a baton and swaggers like a drum majorette while the Assistant beats out a march on the percussion.)*
That is a silly swagger.

HE CANDIDATE:
I'm sorry, Sir.

HE MASTER:
Why do you swagger like a drum majorette instead of an officer?

HE CANDIDATE:
I don't have the rank.

HE MASTER *(Reverently, to a shimmer on the percussion, he pulls out a star from a box at the side of the stage.):*
I promote you. What are you?

HE CANDIDATE *(Looking at the star as he pins it on her shoulder):*
A star ...

HE MASTER:
A star is the symbol of a general. Swagger with the star like a general! *(She tries unsuccessfully.)* With more dignity! You are

111

the master of planning, the great crusader! *(She tries with mor*
dignity.) You are the defender of peace!

THE CANDIDATE *(At the front of the stage, to the audience):*
I swear to defend the country ... *(The Assistant breathes a low*
whisper of applause.) with all of the swagger sticks at my com
mand ... *(More applause from the Assistant.)*

THE MASTER *(Raising his swagger stick):*
Against all swagger sticks?

THE CANDIDATE *(Raising her swagger stick against his):*
Against all other swagger sticks!

THE MASTER *(Gesturing upstage):*
Through the history of combat? *(He stares at her as she looks a*
him for a clue.) In the indivisible past?

THE CANDIDATE *(Puzzled):*
Invisible?

THE MASTER *(Gesturing as the lights go down a little):*
In the forest primeval ... The frontier of promise ... *(The Maste*
begins to test her historically. As usual, she seizes on images o
romantic sensuality from which he tries to break her away.) Yo
enter the wilderness ... *(She hesitates and he motions her into th*
wilderness, repeating): You enter the wilderness! You hack ou
your trails of discovery ... *(She hacks out trails of discovery*
What flickers there in the forest? Fire! Fire! *(She kneels like*
romantic Indian squaw and twirls her swagger stick as if she wer
lighting a fire.) Pocohontas, Red Woman of Fire, you swagger i
fire everywhere ... *(She rises and dances around in a circle, cr*
ing out joyous war whoops which do not please the Master). N
No! You are a dirty squaw sitting in your crude teepee! *(Cha*
tised, she squats down.) You seduce the white man! ... You mi
the races. *(She rises and moves forward.)* You stir up the Mel
ing Pot ... The settlers revolt! They send soldiers into the fore
... They slash down the dark, dripping trees ... *(He moves afte*
her, slashing at her. Startled, the Candidate runs across the stag
She recoils in fear behind a chair, her fingers clutching the back o
the chair as if she were a prisoner in a camp.)

112

Jordon Howard and Jennifer Warren in Edward Call's Production of *The Master,*

HE CANDIDATE:
  The Indian is driven out into reserved camps! *(The Master resents this and drives her on.)*

HE MASTER:
  You escape from the reserved camps ... You join the Native Revolutionaries ... You revolt against the Imperial Invaders!

HE CANDIDATE *(Joyfully):*
  I'm a Minute Man!

HE MASTER *(Pushing her on):*
  You organize in groups ... You train on raw rations ... You practice guerrilla warfare against the Imperial Invaders! *(The Candidate expands her hypnotic dream of a romantic, revolutionary soldier.)*

HE CANDIDATE:
  "One if by land, two if by sea" ...

HE MASTER *(Taking up a role against her to spur her on):*
  I take up the sword of the Imperial Invaders ...

HE CANDIDATE:
  "By the rude bridge that arched the flood" ...

HE MASTER *(Trying desperately to break through):*
  ... To master the romantic, native revolutionaries!

HE CANDIDATE *(Still happy with her fantasy):*
  The shot heard 'round the world! *(A shot is heard on the percussion.)*

HE MASTER *(Recoiling a little):*
  The Imperial Invaders found swords of little use in the National Wilderness ...

HE CANDIDATE:
  The revolutionaries hid behind trees. *(She ducks behind the desk and chair, taking irritating shots from concealment at the master, which makes him angrier.)*

HE MASTER *(Threatening her as he fixes his bayonet in a proud, upright stance):* In our thin red lines we fix bayonets for the charge ...

113

THE CANDIDATE *(From her shelter):*

The Revolutionary sniper in his coonskin shoots you to the ground like flies!

THE MASTER *(Lunging at her in a mechanical march with his bayonet).*
Charge! *(His savage charge reveals the intensity of his anger and she is afraid suddenly. He hurts her with his swagger stick in the charge and she lies on the ground, afraid, making the most of her wound.)* Advance!... Why are you lying there? ... You're in the open line of fire! *(She struggles to get up.)* You've stopped the attack ... Are you retreating? ... Does the yellow streak coil up your back? *(She turns a face of aggressive hatred and cleverness to him and rushes toward him where she mimes the burial of her swagger stick and prepares to explode it.)*

THE CANDIDATE *(As he looks down, puzzled):*

I dig a hole ... Bury my weapon ... *(She puts a package in the hole.)* Light the fuse ... *(She lights the fuse and rushes back up stage.)* 5 - 4 - 3 - 2 - 1! *(A loud BOOM from the percussionist and the Candidate screams at the explosion. The Master jumps with joy pleased that he's breaking through her fantasies.)*

THE MASTER:

Good!... Dynamite!... You invent new weapons for defense.. You blow up my last bridge, my fortress, my headquarters... You flush out my last pocket of resistance ... My ancient redcoats vanish in the distance... You are victorious! *(The Assistant breathes out applause again, but the Master pushes her on.)* You advance to the Civil War! *(Suddenly, improvising her new role with the swagger stick, the Candidate takes the side of the romantic south.)*

THE CANDIDATE:

I parade my colors ... I fire on Fort Sumter!... I fight for the old plantation, for the Mammies who sing us to sleep at night... All over the South we fight for States Rights! *(She lets out a rebel yell.)* Surrender, Yankee!... Wave your white flag! *(She marches against the Master, singing and whistling, "Dixie" ("I wish I was in the land of cotton, etc.") The Master is not pleased. Disgusted with her romantic illusion again, he drives her back.)*

THE MASTER:

Never, never, never! The house is divided against itself ... Lincoln banishes slavery ... You desert from the South ... You fight for the National Eagle! ... *(She stares at him, scared, recoiling from her aggression, instinctively seeking some private shelter.)*

THE MASTER:
Take cover! ... The secret weapon, the Gatling Gun, with its rotating barrels, fires at you 1200 rounds a minute ... *(She staggers and searches desperately for shelter.)* Reinforced by my Sharps Rifles at the Battles of Bull Run ... Run! ... *(She runs and suddenly begins to dig under the table.)*

THE CANDIDATE:
I escape! I escape from your Civil War! ... I dig underground into the future!

THE MASTER *(Upset, as he thinks she is retreating again into her fantasies):*
What are you doing? ... You can't escape ... You can't change wars! ...

THE CANDIDATE *(Digging and hiding under the table):*
I dig my shelter deep underground to coil in against your shells.

THE MASTER *(Furiously):*
Come out of there! ... You conceal yourself like a snake! Where are your defensive weapons?

THE CANDIDATE *(Wavering, but clinging desperately to her situation):*
I bring in my rations ... *(She gets her rations.)* My two thousand calories a day diet of Bulgur Biscuits ... Three and a half gallons of canned water ... *(Worried, as she senses his rage.)* My sanitation kit, including Purity Plastics for human waste ... *(This uncertainty enrages him further and he stalks around the table preparing to attack her. She waves her swagger stick feebly at him in defense of sanctuary.)*

THE MASTER *(He presses the button on the end of his swagger stick. Banging on the table with his swagger stick, he climbs up on the table and stamps on it heavily with his foot.):*
I am the invading fury from the sky — the fire, the gas, the nausea, the heat! ... I filter into your shelter! I vomit all of your Bulgur

115

Buiscuits!... I defecate in your Purity Plastics! I clean out your shelter!

THE CANDIDATE *(Terrified, she rolls out of the shelter and rushes downstage.)*:
Red Alert!... The enemy attacks!... I press the button... *(She does so on the end of her swagger stick.)* The metal birds rise from their silent cold nests ... They fill the air with the sound and fury of destruction! *(Looking up at the excitement of this vision, she recoils suddenly.)* Ah, we're all dying...

THE MASTER *(Going to her)*:
What is it? Who has killed you?

THE CANDIDATE *(Waving her stick feebly)*:
The enemies!... Enemies of the swagger stick...

THE MASTER:
I hear your last wish...

THE CANDIDATE:
Bury me under my swagger stick ... I am in Go Condition ... I circle around and around ... around and around ... around and around ... *(Struggling back into a state of feminine, public aggression, sensing the Master's intense desire.)* I am pursuing ... Happiness! *(Dies, disturbed, wondering if she has failed, twitching a little.)*

THE MASTER *(At her feet, contemplating her, wondering about his role as Master)*:
I bury you with *some* military honors ... The funeral drums pound out their dirge. *(A funeral dirge is heard on the drums.)* I plant your swagger stick in the earth to mark the end of your rest. *(Plants the swagger sticks together in the shape of a cross between her feet.)* You have played out your airy visions of war where all the towers and gates of private fantasies crash down and sleep becomes a radiant dream of dust. Peace ... The Peace that Passeth all Understanding ... Amen. *(His voice has assumed an Evangelist's intensity as he stares at her, trying to force her towards the eagle's vision of power.)* The spirit always moves. Rise! Waste motion is lost devotion. Resurrection! *(She rises slowly as he holds the cross of swagger sticks in his hands, singing "Mine eyes have seen the Glory ... etc.")*

116

THE MASTER *(Sharply)*:
  What glory do you see?

THE CANDIDATE *(Uncertainly)*:
  A presence . . .

THE MASTER *(Impatiently)*:
  Presence?

THE CANDIDATE *(Trembling, staring desperately)*:
  I see . . .

THE MASTER:
  A light?

THE CANDIDATE *(Staring)*:
  Clearer . . .

THE MASTER *(Sharply)*:
  A sky? A sun?

THE CANDIDATE *(Staring)*:
  No . . .

THE MASTER:
  A figure?

THE CANDIDATE:
  Yes . . . I think . . .

THE MASTER:
  A face?

THE CANDIDATE *(Staring uncertainly)*:
  I'm not sure . . .

THE MASTER *(Impatiently)*:
  Listen!

THE CANDIDATE *(Listening intently)*:
  No words . . .

THE MASTER:
  Music?

THE CANDIDATE:
  I can't hear!

117

THE MASTER *(Prodding her into discovery):*
Touch!

THE CANDIDATE:
No feeling!

THE MASTER:
What do you see?

THE CANDIDATE *(Slowly, shuddering):*
Invisible . . .

THE MASTER *(Sharply):*
Failure! *(She is huddled tensely in her anguish.)* We must change . . .
Take off your uniform . . . It is time for the autobiography of en-
lightenment . . . Relax . . . Take a smoke . . .

THE CANDIDATE *(Subdued, humble, taking a cigarette that he lights and
gives to her.):*
Thank you, sir.

THE MASTER:
Sit down . . . *(She sits down.)*
Comfortable? Not too comfortable . . . Sit on the edge of the chair.
(She moves to the edge of the chair.)

THE MASTER *(He takes a cigar.):*
The story of how I became a Master. *(As he talks and moves around,
he smokes and gestures with the cigar.)* I began at birth, a baby
of inevitable strength, an extrovert from the start. Naturally, my
immigrant parents conceived me as a Master. Out of twisted
English was to come a professional man. Everyone has the right
to be a Master — if he has the right equipment: I.Q., Stable Per-
sonality, Grit, Will, and the rest . . . I was an ugly boy, staring at
success, my ugliness a glare in the mirror. I broke all mirrors! In
the dark hours of the morning I sold a city of papers. I earned a
banquet, a medal, a round trip to the towers of New York. The
skyscrapers shattered my eyes. Man could do that! I sold my way
through schools and college in a wonder of facts. My ear was deaf
only to foreign languages. I polished my English, my American
even more. I learned the morality of manners. I walked on the
curb side of women. I studied love with many women until I

married one. Came the war. I served as an officer ... I dreamt of far-off victories for which I thirsted at a dried-up desk. After my discharge from the army, I sank and struggled up in quicksand studies. The hooded colors of the Ph.D. flared over my shoulders! At last I was a Philosopher! Money flowed to me through business, government research, the marvelous labyrinths of lucid teamwork. Landlord, I raised my mansion in the suburbs! ... Then one vacation we flew to Europe. My children stared at Old Masters in the museums. They groveled in the beautiful cathedrals and the lobbies of Baroque opera houses. After our return came the awakening, the sense of American Power. We were old! Our faces were wrinkled with freedom. It was time to be young again, eternally young, eternally westward. To stop at the halfway house is not the home of the Master. I must teach, not Oriental or European, but risk the extreme like an American. Candidates would come to me like rivers flowing to their goal. Masters would create Mastery! Preserve the republican sceptre of achievement! Achieve the proud world of the lonely Master! Let the great rivers of enlightenment — Columbia, Colorado, Hudson, Missouri, Rio Grande, Mississippi — flow with the fury of knowledge in the Master's veins, his mind, his will! *(He crushes out the cigar to end his autobiography and contemplates the Candidate in silence for a moment. Percussion music is heard. Waiting, the Candidate stares at him. He gives no orders. It is up to her. Finally, she begins her autobiography.)*

THE CANDIDATE:

My beginning was comfort and security ... We lived in a big house thirty miles away from the city, deep in a lovely woods ... White birch trees glistened along the drive. ... The Birds of Paradise soared out of our garden in their orange-flame colors ... My father disappeared down the freeway every morning to his work ... He was a tower of strength in that city ... When he came home tired at night he was received like a king ... His drink was ready ... My mother was dressed up in her pale housecoat ... If he wasn't too tired, he fired up a happy cloud of smoke over the charcoal broiler in the backyard ... He cooked the best steak you ever tasted ... My mother was devoted to her home and children ... She ran everything on the slickest timetable you ever saw, decorating, cooking, buying, visiting her clubs, taking us to ballet lessons after school ...

She was artistic too... She'd always choose a wallpaper that knocked your eye out... and she had a real touch for antique furniture... Her favorite possession was her four poster spool bed with a rose silk canopy... She used to say, "I feel like a Queen sleeping in that bed!" ...My sister and I invented the games of romance... We colored boxes into castles... We turned our pets into knights and lords and princes... We steamed the bathroom mirrors into reflections of palaces... There were so many bathrooms in that house... You could lock the door and be alone with your dreams of beauty. *(She pauses and looks at the Master.)*

THE MASTER:
Continue...

THE CANDIDATE:
When I left home, I wanted to be successful too... If you want something badly enough you can still get it in this country... At fifteen I walked down the high school corridor in a tight sweater and the boys whistled at me... I knew from the mirrors that I had a face and a body... So I began to enter all of the beauty contests ...In college I was voted Sorority Princess... Then I won the Annual Rose Competition... I learned how to walk in a bathing suit with the control that is graceful, but not too sexual... I learned how to sing popular songs well enough to pass the talent tests... I learned how to wear clothes and smile at the right people ...After winning the state competition, I walked around in the clouds... They were going to send me east!... Suddenly, I was there, in Atlantic City! ...We stayed in a big hotel where we were guarded like crown jewels...I was first in the bathing suit competition, but only fourth in the talent tests... The jury asked me questions... One juror asked: "What would you do if you found your boy friend with another girl?"... I answered, "I'd knock him over!"... I couldn't believe it when they called my name... I walked down the runway in a daze... The band was playing... The crown was on my head... That was my night of victory!... I went out to dedicate parking lots... I modeled and sold the latest fashions... I waved with Mayors and Governors in parades... I cut the ribbons at the opening of new shopping centers... I learned to dedicate...

120

THE MASTER *(Breaking in):*
  You learned you are the ideal average woman.

THE CANDIDATE:
  Yes, Sir.

THE MASTER:
  You have lived the ideal average.

THE CANDIDATE:
  Yes, Sir.

THE MASTER:
  The Master is not average. Begin again.

THE CANDIDATE:
  I don't understand ...

THE MASTER:
  Rise above the average! Use your vision!

THE CANDIDATE:
  How?

THE MASTER:
  When nothing makes sense, choose American Nonsense.

THE CANDIDATE *(Puzzled):*
  Nonsense?

THE MASTER:
  Make a choice!

THE CANDIDATE:
  Give me a clue.

THE MASTER *(As the percussionist pounds out the jazz rhythms building
    up and up in tempo, the Master leads the Candidate through the
    riddle and the baseball sequence to the image of the eagle.):*
  Why does the lonely chicken cross the road?

THE CANDIDATE *(Slowly):*
  To get ... to the green pastures ...

THE MASTER:
  Why does the road cross the lonely chicken?

THE CANDIDATE *(Beginning to participate in the game)*:
To pasture in the green get.

THE MASTER:
Why does the cross road lonely on the chicken?

THE CANDIDATE:
To green in the pastures gotten!

THE MASTER:
Why does the freight train howl in the night?

THE CANDIDATE *(Moving towards him, as their movements become increasingly dance-like to the jazz rhythms.)*:
To cover the lonely distance.

THE MASTER:
Where is the only entrance to the freeway?

THE CANDIDATE:
At the door of the cage.

THE MASTER:
Between beer and whisky, where does the drunkard drown?

THE CANDIDATE *(Beginning to be drawn out of herself)*:
In the glass of himself . . .

THE MASTER *(More exultantly, now that he is beginning to move her out of herself)*:
What dream does the dreamer dream at Dream Farm?

THE CANDIDATE:
The echoing bird is not the real singer.

THE MASTER:
How does the blind man cross the road while the deer stands still

THE CANDIDATE:
The music of the feet commands the eye.

THE MASTER:
Why is Mary, Mary quite contrary?

IE CANDIDATE *(Faster and faster tempo as the Assistant builds up a jazz salvo on the percussion):*
Because she's hairy, hairy, hairy!

IE MASTER:
What does the undertaker say to the bones?

IE CANDIDATE *(Breaking out joyfully now):*
Rise you old burdens, rise and shine!

IE MASTER:
How does the cheese eat the cheeseburger?

IE CANDIDATE:
Lettuce to go, pickled with relish!

IE MASTER:
When the leaves of fall *fall,* how does spring *spring?*

IE CANDIDATE:
The jackrabbit jumper is a Jim Dandy!

HE MASTER:
What is the pasture of the National Pastime?

HE CANDIDATE:
Cows of the world, unite!

HE MASTER *(Satisfied in her progress with the riddles and jazz dance steps, he takes her through a nonsense baseball sequence still leading her to a recognition of the power and force of the Eagle.):*
Fly American!

HE CANDIDATE *(Happily):*
Screw Zen Buddhism! *(The Assistant calls out "Hot Dogs! Root Beer! etc." as the Master picks up a baseball bat and moves toward the plate behind which the candidate is standing.):*

HE MASTER:
Play ball! *(The Candidate signals strike one before the Master has swung.)* You blind or something? Put on your glasses! *(The Candidate puts on a pair of dark glasses.)* That's better. Look 'em over.

THE CANDIDATE *(As the Master looks at an obviously high ball)*:
Strike two!

THE MASTER:
You're blind as a bat!

THE CANDIDATE *(Wildly)*:
Strike two and a half!

THE MASTER *(Threatening her with the bat)*:
You're crazy, you psycho!

THE CANDIDATE:
Strike three!

THE MASTER:
Who's paying you? What country club are you gonna buy?

THE CANDIDATE *(Jerking her thumb over her shoulder like an umpire*
Out of the game!

THE MASTER:
You rich crook!

THE CANDIDATE:
Out of the stadium! Out of the city!

THE MASTER:
You beer-busted, broken-down bum!

THE CANDIDATE *(Standing up to him)*:
Out of the country!

THE MASTER:
Up the umpires!

THE CANDIDATE:
Down the fans!

THE MASTER *(He puts the bat away and laughs suddenly, delighted*
her real progress.):
Precise playing.

THE CANDIDATE:
Lovely feeling.

E MASTER:
Name projects.

E CANDIDATE (*Climbing up on the table, approaching the vision of power*):
Saint! Midas! Titan! Mercury! Venus!

E MASTER:
Rise above gravity!

E CANDIDATE (*Exultantly*):
Rule with radiation!

E MASTER (*He has brought her through the nonsense sequence and brings her now to the vision of the Eagle of Power.*):
What is the true American?

E CANDIDATE:
He moves, he flies, he travels forever.

E MASTER (*Intently*):
Describe his motion.

E CANDIDATE:
Restless motion.

E MASTER:
With wings?

E CANDIDATE (*Crying out*):
Eagle wings!

E MASTER:
What kind of eagle?

E CANDIDATE (*Exultantly*):
A Golden Eagle because he flies against the sky. He swoops in the mountains showing his even black color. When he wheels, the flash of white on his tail and the mark of gold on his hind neck give him his grace. No vulture, a Golden Eagle, he soars and hooks into the burning sky!

E MASTER (*Commanding*):
Show me the flight of the Golden Eagle! (*Slowly the Candidate begins to move her torso. Her neck twitches. She begins to dance the*

125

Flight of the Golden Eagle to percussion music. There is a ris
sense of exhilaration, of soaring upward, of powerful flight. Th
the flight begins to falter and she slips down from the table.)

THE MASTER *(Satisfied, he pushes her on to the final test.):*
Rest ... You have begun. Now you must end ...

THE CANDIDATE:
End?

THE MASTER:
How does death approach?

THE CANDIDATE *(Staring at him anxiously, she whispers):*
In disguise.

THE MASTER:
Which disguise?

THE CANDIDATE:
The disguise of old age.

THE MASTER:
Put on the disguise of old age. *(The Assistant brings her the hat*
old age.)

THE MASTER:
You are old, you are sick. What is your disease?

THE CANDIDATE *(Whispering):*
It is incurable.

THE MASTER:
What is it called?

THE CANDIDATE:
Old age.

THE MASTER *(Putting on his hat of old age):*
I am old, too. Where do we live?

THE CANDIDATE:
Away from our children.

THE MASTER *(They are both playing an old couple, but the Maste*
still leading her, testing her through the old age sequence.):

126

We want our independence. We don't want to be a burden to our children.

HE CANDIDATE:

We live by ourselves with other old folk in Moon City. We don't let people in Moon City until they're over the hill.

HE MASTER:

We can have a lot of fun if we just don't sit down and die.

HE CANDIDATE:

We sleep a lot. I can still sleep up a storm, especially if it's raining.

HE MASTER:

We see our children once in a while when they come to visit.

HE CANDIDATE *(As they wander along in their isolation)*:

We go out to eat once a week at the Woodthrift — soup, roast beef, carrots, mashed potatoes, pomegranite Jello, and Sanka for a dollar and twenty-five cents.

HE MASTER:

Sometimes we go to a prayer meeting.

HE CANDIDATE:

Hear a lecture.

HE MASTER:

Walk along to see who's old ...

HE CANDIDATE:

We're very social in our security.

HE MASTER:

At the Senior Citizens' Center, they have square dancing. *(They begin to dance and they are breathing heavily at the end of a few steps.)* It's a leisure world. Old age should be a long vacation.

HE CANDIDATE:

A sea voyage!

OTH:

Bon voyage!

THE CANDIDATE:
   In St. Petersburg, we can have our blood pressure taken for thirty-five
   cents in a streetcorner booth.

THE MASTER:
   Or play shuffleboard on 107 courts. *(Plays shuffleboard.)*

THE CANDIDATE:
   I like to listen to the free band concerts.

THE MASTER:
   We love children, but when you get old, you can't have them around
   all the time.

THE CANDIDATE:
   People are growing older. We're very old and we're still alive.

THE MASTER:
   We can live on less than $5,000 a year.

THE CANDIDATE:
   If we're segregated.

THE MASTER:
   What we do is sleep good and late.

THE CANDIDATE:
   Good and late in the morning.

THE MASTER:
   Sleep is good for old people. Early to bed, late to rise ...

THE CANDIDATE:
   Makes the old folks old and wise.

THE MASTER *(Cackles):*
   Sometimes we miss the children.

THE CANDIDATE:
   We get lonely for them.

THE MASTER:
   But we are lonely together.

THE CANDIDATE:
   We're starting a new life.

Robert Benson and Erica Rosqui in Herbert Blau's production of *The Master*, The Actor's Workshop, San Francisco.

THE MASTER:
We're together. Forever.

THE CANDIDATE:
Forever.

THE MASTER:
Forever.

THE CANDIDATE:
Forever.

THE MASTER:
Forever... *(The "forevers" get louder and louder until they are screaming at each other like eagles, then they fade out slowly. There is a long pause.)*

THE MASTER:
Take off the wig! *(She lifts it off slowly and he says exultantly)* Old age flies away from you like the eagle gliding over the white spindrift of the wave! We begin...

THE CANDIDATE *(Slowly)*:
We end?

THE MASTER:
I am the Candidate.

THE CANDIDATE:
I am the Master?

THE MASTER:
We begin! We end! *(The Assistant pulls down a window shade on which is painted a large bald-headed eagle staring fiercely at the audience. In one claw is an olive branch, in the other claw the slogan, "E Pluribus Unum." The final Eagle Marriage Ceremony begins.)*

THE CANDIDATE *(With growing recognition)*:
I am the Mistress...

THE MASTER *(Bowing)*:
We Candidates salute you.

THE CANDIDATE *(With a growing smile)*:
I am the Mistress of American Power!

THE MASTER:
We honor you, oh Mistress of Power.

THE CANDIDATE *(With a gesture of power)*:
Have a cigar. *(The Master selects a cigar.)* Sit down. *(She knocks the lighter off the table so that he reaches to pick it up.)* Light it! *(He does so.)* Shoulders back! The proud position! On the edge of the chair! *(He moves to the edge of the chair, sitting there rigidly, puffing out a cloud of smoke.)* I can't stand the stink of a cigar. Put it out! *(He crushes out the cigar. She commands in a low, intense voice.)* Fly American Eagle, fly for me! *(She invokes the eagle as the Master rises and the Assistant begins to play the final Eagle Marriage Ceremony on the percussion. The movements of this ritual Eagle Dance are intense and sensuous, but they break out occasionally from the physical sense of a marriage ceremony to repeat earlier satirical elements in the play.)* White Eagle on your high nest in the dead pine tree, fly to me! Lone eagle floating on blocks of ice down rivers, give me your mastery. Fly to me!

THE MASTER *(Moving toward her)*:
Proud eagle guarding our dream, "Out of the Many, One."

THE CANDIDATE:
Bless this search from youth through age to power.

TOGETHER:
To power! To power! To power!

THE MASTER:
Bald eagle in your burning uight. I take this woman to love, honor, and obey.

THE CANDIDATE:
I take this man to cherish the mastery of power.

THE MASTER:
Obey . . .

THE CANDIDATE:
Cherish . . .

THE MASTER:
Obey . . .

THE CANDIDATE:
  Cherish . . .

THE MASTER *(Their arms and bodies are whirling now in wild, opposed motions, his up, and hers down.)*:
  Through the bright air . . .

THE CANDIDATE:
  The white clouds . . .

THE MASTER:
  The lightning . . .

THE CANDIDATE:
  The thunder . . .

THE MASTER:
  In the glory of flight . . .

THE CANDIDATE:
  Moving together . . . *(They move together.)*

THE MASTER:
  In the dance of flesh . . .

THE CANDIDATE:
  Moving! In the glory of our dancing flesh!

TOGETHER *(There is a jazz sequence as they dance together sensuously.)*:
  Moving in the glory! Glory! Glory!
  Moving in the glory of our dancing flesh!

THE MASTER:
  Fierce eagle clutching your olive branch,
  Bless the power and the glory of our marriage.

THE CANDIDATE *(Preening her claws)*:
  Bright eagle with your furious eye,
  Tear with your claws for the glory.

TOGETHER:
  Tear, tear for the glory!

THE MASTER:
  Bold eagle bless this union.

131

THE CANDIDATE:
Proud eagle bless this union.

TOGETHER *(In a fierce whisper):*
Bless! Bless! Bless!

THE MASTER *(As the dance reflects the military sequence and the Assistant plays martial music on the percussion):*
Brave eagle with your brilliant eye,
Guard our freedom!

THE CANDIDATE:
Fierce eagle in your burning flight,
Guard our freedom!

TOGETHER *(Fiercely):*
Freedom! Freedom! Freedom!

THE CANDIDATE:
Eagle to eagle . . .

THE MASTER:
Joined together . . .

THE CANDIDATE:
Praise the hunting weather!

TOGETHER:
Praise the marriage of power! Praise!
(She has leapt up on him and slides down his side into an embrace as the play ends with a final salvo on the percussion and an abrupt blackout.)

THE END

The
Black
President

A Song-Scenario for the Stage

To Joan Littlewood

A Note on the Form of the Play:

As indicated in the term, "song-scenario," the play combines the techniques of film, stage, and musical theatre. If the theatre is to maintain its individuality and power, in competition with the range of the best films, the theatre must experiment with the rapid cutting and close focus of film techniques. At the same time, the unique power of the stage, the direct contact with the audience and the greater opportunities for word and song, must not be neglected.

The tempo of this "song-scenario" is very important and must flow with the pace of a film through the transitions. There are, of course, no pauses between the various scenes. The scenes are numbered, as in film continuity, to make the formal sequence more apparent and to facilitate rehearsal. Many of the film episodes are documentary and actually occurred, but they should be filmed for the play with appropriate style so that the direct, simple, theatrical aim of the play is preserved.

The whole work is conceived for the new theatre of which Joan Littlewood has dreamed and for which she has fought in her best productions.

"Oui, j'ai les yeux fermés à votre lumière. Je suis une bête, une nègre. Mais je puis être sauvé. Vous êtes de faux nègres, vous, maniaques, féroces, avares. Marchand, tu es nègre; magistrat, tu es nègre; général, tu es nègre; empereur, vieillé démangeaison, tu es nègre; tu as bu d'une liqueur non taxée, de la fabrique de Satan."

Rimbaud, *Une Saison en Enfer*

CAST (In order of their appearance.)

1

(A film shot on a front, scrim curtain shows a 19th century slave ship sailing across the ocean. Before the curtain, the chorus of crew members of "The Black President" are cleaning their guns, etc. They sing):

CHORUS

Where's that ship gonna sail?
Sail here, sail there, sail everywhere.
Sail, man, sail that *Black President,*
Sail here, sail there, sail everywhere!

(At the end of the opening chorus, the scrim curtain is drawn up to reveal the Tea Room of the House of Commons in London, fronting on the Thames. It is a day when Question Time is scheduled in the House. Two waitresses, a Spanish girl, Carla Davida, and an older English woman, Fanny Boles, are preparing last-minute cafeteria arrangements for the visitors to the House. They are assisted by a teen-age helper, Johnny Tennon.)

FANNY *(Calling)*:
More cups, Johnny.

JOHNNY:
Coming. *(He brings the cups.)*

CARLA *(To Fanny)*:
You have many visitors this afternoon?

FANNY:
Sure, love, it's Question Day. Any member of the house can ask questions of government officials.

JOHNNY:
Lots of people come to hear the questions from the Stranger's Gallery.

CARLA:
What is Stranger's Gallery?

FANNY:
The balcony where visitors sit.

JOHNNY:

The questions are listed in an Order Paper.

CARLA *(Puzzled)*:

Order Paper?

JOHNNY:

Don't worry. You'll catch on.
(He and Fanny sing, "Question Time in the House.")

FANNY and JOHNNY *(Singing together)*:

The Order Paper's printed.
It's Question Time in the House.

JOHNNY *(Spoken recitative to music)*:

"To ask the Minister of Colonial Affairs—what is the government's long-range policy in Africa?"

FANNY *(Reading the answer satirically)*:

"Naturally, every time there is an interest to the extent shown to the House today on this question, it is a matter for deliberation as to how opportunities can be taken for the question to be further ventilated and discussed." And I stress the word, *ventilated,* even though I don't know what the hell it means!

FANNY and JOHNNY:

They'll question and they'll question
Till the questions cause congestion,
Oh, it's Question Time in the House.
(Carla joins in)
Yes, the Order Paper's printed,
And it's Question Time in the House.

JOHNNY *(Spoken recitative again)*:

"To ask the Secretary of State for the Home Department, if he will impress upon the Commission of Police for the Metropolis the undesirability of sending police dogs to political or trade-union meetings."

FANNY:

"I assure the Right Honorable Member I will undertake to inquire about the proper training and manners of police dogs."

137

FANNY and JOHNNY and CARLA:
   They'll question and they'll question
   Till the questions cause congestion,
   Oh, it's Question Time in the House.

   See, the Order Paper's printed,
   And it's Question Time in the House.

FANNY *(Spoken):*
   "To ask the Lord Privy Seal if he will take further action to minimise
      the risk of war by spreading Polaris submarine bases to other
      member-countries of the North Atlantic Treaty Organization, so
      as to decrease the vulnerability of the Western deterrent."

JOHNNY:
   "Yes, we are always taking actions further and further,
   Sir, in connection with the *de*-terrent."

FANNY and JOHNNY and CARLA:
   They'll question and they'll question
   Till the questions cause congestion,
   Oh, it's Question Time in the House.

3

CARLA *(After the song, she sighs):*
   My English is so slow . . .

FANNY:
   You sound fine. Make your customers repeat if you can't understand
      them.

CARLA:
   I don't like to do that.

JOHNNY:
   They can wait. *(Reflecting)* You know I'd like to go to Spain — all
      those ads in the papers about the Costa . . . What's it called?

CARLA:
   Costa Brava.

JOHNNY:
   Must be lovely. All that sun. Where do you live?

CARLA:

In Madrid. My father teaches there. But we don't go to the Costa
Brava. Most Spaniards do not have the money to go.

FANNY *(This starts her off.)*:

I used to work for a lawyer who went on vacation to that Costa
Bruvo, or whatever you call it. After his wife died, he got married
again to a young girl. Twenty years younger, she was. I couldn't
stand her.

JOHNNY *(Aside, to Carla)*:

Watch out. You encourage her, she'll yack your head off.

FANNY:

I did my work, mind you. She was after me all the time. Like I was
a stick. Giving me orders as if I was a piece of wood. "Don't forget to hoover under the bed." Her husband comes to me and says,
"Don't mind her, Fanny. Just do what she says. I'll see you get
paid extra. She's not well, you know." I can't work for sick people,
can I? They're after you all the time. One afternoon, I'm drinking
a cup of tea in the kitchen. She starts to swear at me. "Damn it,
you didn't hoover under the bed," she screams. That was it. I went
to her husband. "I'm sorry," I says, "She's giving me ulcers..."

JOHNNY *(Bored and glad for the interruption)*:

Here comes someone.

*(Two young colored men enter, a Nigerian in colorful robes, and
a West Indian.)*

FANNY *(To Carla)*:

We get a lot of blacks. Mostly African students. Their teachers send
'em around to learn how Parliament works.

4

WEST INDIAN *(To Nigerian)*:

Christmas in London is terrifying. I spent the last one with an
English family who locked me up for three days with television.

139

NIGERIAN:

It's a closed-shop affair.

WEST INDIAN:

Everyone retires into their houses in units of three or four.

NIGERIAN:

There isn't much joy when people do that.

WEST INDIAN:

At home in the West Indies, chaps get merry and have a drink. The
go out and visit each other's homes.

NIGERIAN *(Sighing):*

I was given so many presents, I lost all my money buying gifts i
return.

WEST INDIAN:

In my country, they prefer the visits. It's more friendly. They giv
you a drink, even if it's a drink of water.

NIGERIAN:

I gave my landlady a lamp made out of a wine bottle.

WEST INDIAN:

Did she like it?

NIGERIAN:

I think it upset her. She likes a very methodical Christmas. She'
a Methodist.

WEST INDIAN:

It would be better to have Christmas in the summer here.

NIGERIAN:

Why?

WEST INDIAN:

The weather would be better. People would want to go out and visi
each other.

TOGETHER *(They sing "The English Should Have Christmas in Sum
mer.")*

The English should have Christmas in Summer,
The weather might be better then.
Religion wouldn't be a bore
And presents wouldn't be a chore,
For chaps could concentrate on being friends.

The English should have Christmas in Summer,
It would be much more fun for them.
The businessmen might think it rash
For it's the time when they make cash,
But chaps could concentrate on being friends.

(After the song, they turn away to one of the tables. Jackburn enters, takes some food, and goes to another table. Hooper and his sister also enter.)

WEST INDIAN *(Motioning to Jackburn):*
He's on time.

NIGERIAN :
Let's hope there won't be any trouble on the river.

WEST INDIAN :
Remember, if there's trouble, we wait.

NIGERIAN :
We're students visiting the House of Commons.

WEST INDIAN *(Smiling):*
That's the truth.

5

(At their table, Hooper turns to his sisters.)

HOOPER:
A good many blacks in the House today.

MISS HOOPER :
Students most likely.

HOOPER *(With a gesture towards Jackburn):*
He's a bit old for a student, though I suppose some of them need a
longer time for their education.

MISS HOOPER *(Looking at Jackburn)*:
Where do you think he's from?

HOOPER:
Who can tell? Either they imitate our clothes, or they wear thos gaudy robes. *(He gestures towards the Nigerian.)*

MISS HOOPER:
I wish they would all wear robes. They're so colorful.

HOOPER *(Smiling)*:
Why don't you write to the Underground officials to put robes or their Jamaican blacks? They like dressing up.

6

JOHNNY *(To Carla, pointing to an American tourist couple, Laura an Peter Temple, who have just entered)*:
American tourists. We get swamped with 'em.

CARLA:
How can you tell they're American?

JOHNNY *(Smiling)*:
Big cameras growing out of 'em. Loud voices.

FANNY *(To Carla)*:
Loud voices are better than not saying anything. Watch out for thei cameras though. When you clear off the dishes, you're likely t bump into 'em. I hurt my nose on a camera the other day.
(The Americans take some food and sit down at a table.)

LAURA:
I love the way they all bow to the Mace.

PETER:
It's a custom, dear. The Mace is the symbol of authority. It show the power of government is in the House of Commons and not i the King or Queen.

LAURA:
They have so many traditions. Why do the MP's on the front benc put their legs on the table?

ETER:
That's a privilege.

AURA:
Good for their circulation, I suppose. Prevents middle-age blood
clots. *(Peter laughs.)* But I still think it's a little peculiar for a
government leader in grey pants, frock coat, and black shoes to put
his legs up on the table. He wouldn't do it in Washington.

ETER:
They don't have such old traditions in Washington.

AURA:
The custom I like is the uniform of the Ushers.

ETER:
They are grand. I wish you could photograph them.

AURA:
Don't act like an American tourist with a camera.

ETER *(Embarrassed):*
Sh...

7

IGERIAN *(Gesturing to Jackburn):*
Where'd he ever get the name, Moses Jackburn?

EST INDIAN:
From the spiritual they say. The one about Moses freeing his people
from the Pharaoh.

IGERIAN:
Which Pharoah?

EST INDIAN *(Grinning):*
How do I know? I'm a Political Scientist, not a Historian.
(Jackburn signals to them.)

IGERIAN:
Get ready...

(In the course of his work, Johnny passes the glass doors openin, onto the river. He stops, transfixed.)

JOHNNY:

Look! That funny little ship up the river.

FANNY:

There's a big civil rights meeting going on over there.

JOHNNY:

Some of those demonstrators must have launched it.

FANNY:

It's sailing this way. *(Carla has come to see.)*

JOHNNY:

Ships can't land here.

(Jackburn shoulders past them, through the door, and out on th promenade towards the ship.)

FANNY *(Staring at Jackburn)*:

Where's that black think he's going?

JOHNNY *(Calling after Jackburn)*:

Hey, you're not supposed to go out there.

(The West Indian and the Nigerian have produced guns fro beneath their coats. One moves to guard the door that leads to th river promenade; the other moves to guard the door leading int the House.)

NIGERIAN:

Please, ladies and gentlemen, don't be alarmed.

WEST INDIAN:

We don't want your money.

NIGERIAN:

Keep your seats, please. No one will be hurt. In a moment, Captai Jackburn will talk to you.

JOHNNY *(Sneaking a look towards the river, he says to Carla)*:

Blacks pouring off the ship. They're running towards the entrance to the House!

NIGERIAN *(Swinging around):*
Sit down, please.

(Johnny sits down reluctantly. The sound of running footsteps is heard. Indistinct orders are shouted. After a moment, Jackburn re-enters. He has on parts of a uniform now, particularly a cap and an armband. The Nigerian and West Indian have also been putting on armbands.)

MISS HOOPER *(To her brother):*
Are they pirates?

HOOPER:
Couldn't do much in that egg shell of a ship.

LAURA *(To Peter, pointing to Jackburn's cap):*
Isn't he wearing an American army cap?

9

JACKBURN:
Stay quietly where you are and you will be perfectly safe.

HOOPER *(Getting up):*
You can't hold us here.

JACKBURN *(Ironically, as the Nigerian moves towards Hooper):*
Please, no violence. Let us remember we are all ex-Christians. *(Hooper sits down slowly.)* That's better . . . You will excuse our uniforms. I'm afraid we are not too well equipped.

CARLA:
What do you want?

JACKBURN *(Turning to her):*
A foreign girl. Where do you come from?

CARLA:
Spain.

145

JACKBURN *(Reflecting)*:
Spain, that's different. *(Then, mockingly)* You came to learn the English language, the fountainhead of liberty.

LAURA *(To Peter)*:
Be careful. He's mad.

JACKBURN *(Overhearing)*:
Mad ... That's a proposition to be considered. We're absurd figures really. Melodrama everywhere nowadays. *(He reels off a list of cities rapidly and sarcastically, like a train announcer)* London, New York, Paris, Rome, Moscow, Peking, Shanghai, Tokyo, Chicago, Montreal, Buenos Aires, Madrid, Singapore, Hong Kong, Berlin, Vienna, Calcutta, Bucharest, Warsaw, Budapest, Hiroshima .. So many cities. So much violence.

MISS HOOPER *(The stern, courageous old maid)*:
Really, isn't this rather silly? We survived the war here in London. We had to accept things then. If you wish to do something irrational, get on with it.

HOOPER *(Feeling the need to support her)*:
She's quite right, you know. If you have some absurd scheme in mind ...

WEST INDIAN *(Talking to someone outside the door, then calling to Jackburn)*:
They're in the House.

JACKBURN:
Everything all right?

WEST INDIAN *(Grinning)*:
No trouble at all.

JACKBURN:
Good. *(He turns to leave)*:

HOOPER:
Wait! You can't leave us here.

PETER:
What do you expect us to do?

146

JACKBURN:

What do I expect? *(Ironically)* To be torn to pieces by members of
the House of Commons like some Black Orpheus. That's rather
old-fashioned ... The bones don't sing any more. We don't really
believe in resurrection, do we? That grave is a little too welcome.
It's dark in there, a final, comforting blackness. But, maybe,
there's a light somewhere, one little light, maybe right here in the
House of Commons. Not a big glare, not a sun up in the sky as
hot as a bomb, but a little light, enough to get up by in the morning
and look at ourselves in the mirror. *(He sings, "Maybe Somewhere
There's A Little Light".)*

> That grave is a little too welcome,
> Too cold under earth's floor.
> The bones don't sing any more.

> Maybe somewhere there's a little light,
> Not a big glare, not a sun
> In the sky as hot as a bomb,
> But enough to see by, a new world to be won.

> Maybe somewhere there's a little light,
> A little love, a little human heat,
> Not that sky with its burning cloud,
> But some faith in people you meet.

(The West Indian and the Nigerian join in):

> That grave is a little too welcome,
> Too cold under earth's floor.
> The bones don't sing any more.

> Maybe somewhere there's a little light,
> Not a big glare, not a sun
> In the sky as hot as a bomb,
> But enough to see by, a new world to be won.

(He turns and starts through the door.)

HOOPER *(Calling again)*:
Wait!

JACKBURN *(Mockingly, as he pauses at the door)*:
Wait ... The history of man in one word. *Wait!*

(He disappears through the door.)

WEST INDIAN:

Take it easy folks, take it easy. Stay where you are.

10

(After 9, a quick blackout. 10 opens in the House. No additiona. scenery. The Speaker of the House is seen sitting in his wig in his official chair under the canopy at the head of the table. Beside him stands a Negro in a haphazard uniform with a rifle and a grin on his face. The Speaker is squirming and staring indignantly at the large handsome, black and white flag that is descending on the stage. The flag serves as background and a film screen for the scenes outside the Tea Room. As the flag descends, Jackburn is standing at attention at stage right, saluting the flag. His crew members are also on stage saluting. After the flag is lowered, Jackburn turns to address the House.)

JACKBURN:

We launched our ship here in a civil rights demonstration. We raised our flag here in the House of Commons, the birthplace of parliamentary government in the West. London is our first Port of Honor Successive Ports of Honor will be announced upon arrival. Our purpose is simple. We wish to remind the great governments of the guilt of the past and the needs of a future which can be created only by bold and just action. Our ship is a replica of the slave ships that sailed from Africa to America. Below decks are the slaver's pens and the chains. We sail this ship in dedication to black freedom. We plead for the unity of black peoples throughout the world, but we do not set black against white. We raise our flag in the name of racial equality, peace, and freedom in a world where Nationalism has become absurd. We sail in the slow, black ship of slavery to show you that the past must not be forgotten, that the future must be different if man is to survive. *(He sings with his crew, "Across The Sea We Sail.")*

JACKBURN:

> Across the sea we sail
> Until the world of white

Sees through its twisted glass
The black world of night.

THE CREW *(Joining in):*

    Old Dame Freedom's a hag.
    Tear off her mask of white.
    Raise the Black President's flag!

BLACKBURN:

    In the name of freedom,
    We sail the open sea
    To every Port of Honor
    In our ship of slavery.

THE CREW:

    Old Dame Freedom's a hag.
    Tear off her mask of white.
    Raise the Black President's flag!

BLACKBURN:

    Across the sea we sail
    Until the world of white
    Sees through its twisted glass
    The black world of night.

BLACKBURN and CREW:

    Come on, old Dame Freedom.
    Tear off your mask of white.
    Raise the Black President's flag!

11

(After a blackout, the lights come up immediately. 11 is a film sequence, a television commentary on the voyage of "The Black President." A television commentator comes on with a microphone. A camera is focused on him. Note: If it is more convenient, the commentator can be shown on film, so that the entire sequence is on film.)

TELEVISION COMMENTATOR:

Ladies and gentlemen, BBC Television brings you a special program on *The Black President.* Its captain, Moses Jackburn, and his crew of blacks are still barricaded in the Tea Room of the House with several hostages, visitors to Question Time who were trapped by Jackburn's sudden assault. Our first guest is Sir Reginald Denhurst, Lord of the Admiralty. Sir Reginald, can you give us the latest information on *The Black President?*

SIR REGINALD *(Guarded):*

Well, the situation seems somewhat improved. We're holding conferences with Jackburn. He's assured us the hostages will not be harmed.

COMMENTATOR:

Can you tell us what these conferences are about?

SIR REGINALD:

We're trying to determine what will happen to Jackburn and his ship. Of course, Her Majesty's Government cannot permit such violent intrusions into the House. Also, we're seeking to ascertain the international involvement of Jackburn's crew, if you can call them a crew. They've never sailed before.

COMMENTATOR:

Could you clarify that "international involvement," Sir Reginald?

SIR REGINALD:

Well, it seems quite apparent that Jackburn's crew came from various different countries. As for Jackburn himself, as you know it's turned out that he's an American.

COMMENTATOR:

Does the fact that Jackburn is an American make it more difficult for the government?

SIR REGINALD *(Guarded):*

I wouldn't say that. However, we must consider those aspects of this voyage that are apparently political. It seems likely that, despite his immature and impulsive action, Jackburn was motivated by the situation of the colored people in the South.

COMMENTATOR:

But why, then, the international members of his crew?

SIR REGINALD *(With a smile)*:
  From his statement to the House, it seems that one of his motives is
    an effort to abolish Nationalism.

COMMENTATOR:
  What is your view of that, Sir Reginald?

SIR REGINALD *(Cautiously)*:
  Well, Nationalism is Nationalism after all. Of course the world is
    becoming smaller all the time. Nations must move closer together
    if peace is to be attained. Still it seems quite clear that a man is
    born in his own country and must follow his own customs. You
    can't just abolish Nationalism.

COMMENTATOR *(On stage or on film)*:
  Thank you, Sir Reginald. We go now to Africa. In Lagos, Nigeria,
    we'll talk to Nkrume Okolo, the head of the Nigerian Freedom
    Party, and to Michael Daviers, the chairman of the African Uni-
    lateralist Committee.

12 *(A film sequence again.)*

COMMENTATOR *(A white interviewer)*:
  Mr. Okolo, a good many members of Jackburn's crew seem to be
    Africans. Would you care to comment on that?

OKOLO:
  Perhaps they think they make gesture for freedom and independence.

COMMENTATOR:
  You're in favor of this gesture?

OKOLO:
  I didn't say that. We do not know yet where they mean to take this
    strange ship. If they could sail to South Africa, and make Johannes-
    burg one of their Ports of Honor, that might be less of an ad-
    venture.

COMMENTATOR:
  Do you think Jackburn is just an adventurer?

OKOLO: *(Cautiously)*:
  We can't be sure. I feel that we must fight here in Africa first, build

our own countries. It may be less romantic, but it is more practical. *(He sings "Black Africa.")*

> Black Africa is what we need to build,
> > Black Africa first!
> Nation after nation with their power
> > To cool black thirst,
> > Black Africa first!
>
> Throw out the rulers, the exploiters,
> > Black Africa first!
> The time to dream prosperity and peace
> > Comes in the hour
> > After black power.
>
> Black Africa is what we need to build,
> > Black Africa first!

COMMENTATOR:

Thank you, Mr. Okolo. *(Turning to Daviers)* What is your viewpoint of Jackburn's ship, Mr. Daviers?

DAVIERS:

I hope it is true, as reported, that he sails for peace. Perhaps his ship is not as fantastic as it seems.

COMMENTATOR:

Mr. Daviers, some people have wondered at the existence of an African Unilateralist Committee to abolish the bomb, when the African nations don't even have the bomb. Would you care to comment on that?

DAVIERS *(With a smile)*:

I do not believe the bomb respects color, black or white.
(He sings, "Why Can't a Unilateralist Be Black?")
> Why can't a unilateralist be black?
> The atom bomb is not a stone
> And will not fall on white alone.
> Why can't a unilateralist be black?
>
> Why can't a unilateralist be black?
> Is radiation colored snowy white?
> All races melt the same in that hot light.
> Why can't a unilateralist be black?

152

OKOLO *(Who has been waiting indignantly)*:

That's all very well, Daviers, but when colonialism begins to lose power in Africa, you and this dreamer, Jackburn, stop the struggle for independence!

DAVIERS:

That is not true! I merely said if Jackburn sails for peace, perhaps his ship is not as fantastic as it seems.

OKOLO *(Heatedly)*:

You work against the development of African Nationalism!

DAVIERS *(Retorting)*:

I've fought for independence as hard as you have, but I don't want an Africa composed of many little states run by semi-dictators in the name of black liberty. The world's too small for that kind of Africa!

COMMENTATOR *(As Okolo and Daviers argue)*:

Yes, please, gentlemen, could we . . .

OKOLO *(Vehemently)*:

You and Jackburn have fantastic world dreams! Don't you see what will happen? You will be used by those who wish to maintain their colonial power. Help us to build a black Africa first. Then it will be time for your dreams!

DAVIERS:

What about the bomb? Is that black or white?

OKOLO:

You people are obsessed by the bomb. We have no atom bombs in Africa.

DAVIERS:

If there's a war, we'll have them.

COMMENTATOR:

Gentlemen, please . . .

KOLO:

Africa is neutral. Even if another war comes, Africa will have a better chance to survive than the western or eastern countries.

153

DAVIERS:

Survive? Who can survive?

(They sing a brief, fierce duet):

OKOLO:

        Black Africa is what we need to build,
                Black Africa first!
        Black nation after nation with their power
                To cool black thirst,
                Black Africa first!

DAVIERS:

        Why can't a unilateralist be black?
        The atom bomb is not a stone
        And will not fall on white alone.
        Why can't a unilateralist be black?

COMMENTATOR *(Desperately, but smoothly, he cuts off the argument):*
Thank you, Mr. Okolo and Mr. Daviers. After that most interesting
view of influential African opinions of Jackburn's ship, we go now
to the United States to talk to three members of Jackburn's family.
Will you come in New York, please...

13 *(on film)*

NEW YORK COMMENTATOR:

Here in the studio we are fortunate to have three members of Moses
Jackburn's family, his mother, Mrs. Rachel Jackburn; his older
brother, Samuel; and his sister, Bella. The family has requested
that Samuel Jackburn act as their spokesman.

*(The mother, Mrs. Jackburn, sits a little to the rear, a proud, fierce
religious presence. She is a little frightened of the television lights, but
as the scene continues she finds it harder and harder to restrain herself.
The daughter is a more timid, conventional shadow of her mother. The
son, Samuel, who acts as spokesman, is the new, guarded voice of a
Negro seeking entry to the white world of the big cities by political
expediency.)*

COMMENTATOR:

Mr. Jackburn, would you please tell us where your family comes
from?

154

SAMUEL:

Near a small town called Savill in southern Georgia.

COMMENTATOR:

The deep South?

SAMUEL:

That's right, the buried South, but it's changing now.

MRS. JACKBURN (*Unable to restrain herself*):

It change!

SAMUEL:

Please, Mother . . .

COMMENTATOR:

Your father was a farmer?

SAMUEL:

Yes, a tenant farmer, working in the fields all day. As soon as we were old enough, most of us children worked with him.

COMMENTATOR:

You were a large family?

SAMUEL:

Nine of us.

MRS. JACKBURN (*Sharply*):

Ten!

BELLA:

She's counting a baby who died at birth.

MRS. JACKBURN (*Insisting*):

Nobody die! Ten!

SAMUEL:

All right, Mother . . . Ten . . . We lived in a two-room shack, six children in one room, and the rest with our parents in the other room.

MRS. JACKBURN (*Interrupting again*):

I read to the children from The Bible every night.

COMMENTATOR *(Trying to concentrate on Samuel):*
What sort of child was your brother, Moses?

SAMUEL:
We weren't too close. He was younger than me. He used to get into
a little trouble...

MRS. JACKBURN *(Fiercely):*
Not his fault.

BELLA *(Soothingly):*
No one said it was his fault, Mother.

COMMENTATOR:
What sort of trouble?

SAMUEL:
Little things. One day he forged a library card to get books. You
had to be white to get a library card. Somehow he got the reading
bug. So he managed to get a card and forged a signature and
address on it...

MRS. JACKBURN *(Breaking in again):*
I go to see the librarian and tell her about Moses. She nice lady and
agree to give Moses books in secret.

COMMENTATOR:
How old was Moses when you left Georgia?

SAMUEL:
About twelve. We came to New York to live with an uncle. You see
my father was killed in an accident...

MRS. JACKBURN:
No accident!

SAMUEL:
Please, Mother, you agreed...

MRS. JACKBURN:
No accident! Worn out. If you are colored man in South, you shut
your mouth and work hard. He never talk much, but it boil inside
him.

SAMUEL:
Mother . . .

COMMENTATOR *(Interested now, to Mrs. Jackburn):*
How do you mean, *boil inside him?*

MRS. JACKBURN:
Boil with "Yes, Sirs" to the whites, long work without enough money
to feed us, lonely . . .

SAMUEL *(Taking over from his mother with a smooth explanation and
a slight feeling of embarrassment at her lack of sophistication):*
She means, in the South, a colored man lives behind his color all the
time. He can't go in the white world. Everything is separate,
trains, buses, toilets, schools, even movies. So everything becomes
loneliness. My father bottled up everything inside. One day, working in the fields in the hot sun, he collapsed and struck his head . . .

MRS. JACKBURN *(Interrupting):*
No accident! He work to death. It boil inside him!

BELLA:
Please, Mother. You promised to let Samuel . . .

COMMENTATOR *(To Samuel):*
When your family went north, how did Moses feel?

SAMUEL:
He was the bright boy. He wanted to go. When we settled in Harlem,
he worked his way through school.

COMMENTATOR:
What sort of jobs did he do?

SAMUEL *(Shrugging):*
Colored odd-jobs. The ones whites don't want. Garbage, janitor,
ditch digging. But he got to college. Then, he had to go in the
Army.

COMMENTATOR:
Did he conceive the idea of this ship in the Army?

SAMUEL:
I don't know. He didn't like to talk much about the Army. It was
still segregated when he was a soldier.

157

COMMENTATOR:

What do you think of his taking this ship to various "Ports of Honor?"

SAMUEL *(Cautiously; he has been waiting for this question)*:

We are sure that he intends no violence ...

MRS. JACKSON *(Interrupting forcefully)*:

I teach him peace from Bible!

BELLA:

Mother, Samuel is answering ...

COMMENTATOR:

You sympathize, then, with his adventure?

SAMUEL *(A little evasively)*:

We feel that he is sincerely trying to help the cause of the colored man throughout the world. However, we hope that he will come home soon and devote himself to the work that needs to be done for colored people here in the United States.

MRS. JACKBURN *(Unable to restrain herself)*:

He fight for peace!

COMMENTATOR *(Turning to her)*:

Is it true that he was given his name, Moses, because of the spiritual?

MRS. JACKBURN *(There is no restraining her now.)*:

I give him name from the Good Book.

COMMENTATOR *(To Mrs. Jackburn now, as he sees she is the focus of interest, although Samuel and Bella are still trying to restrain her)*:

Did you think of Moses as a liberator of his people?

MRS. JACKBURN *(Fiercely)*:

I hope they all liberators! I teach him to listen as Moses in *Exodus*, when the angel of the Lord appeared unto him in a flame of fire out of the bush!

COMMENTATOR: *(Trying for something with heart to conclude the interview)*:

Mrs. Jackburn, I'm told you liked to sing to your children. I wonder if you'd mind singing us that fine spiritual, "Go Down, Moses."

MRS. JACKBURN:
  I no singer, but I try . . .

BELLA *(Embarrassed)*:
  No, please, mother . . .

SAMUEL *(Also trying to stop his mother)*:
  You promised not to . . .

COMMENTATOR *(Pulling Mrs. Jackburn aside)*:
  Go ahead, Mrs. Jackburn. We'd like very much to hear you.

  *(Mrs. Jackburn starts in a peculiar, harsh, breaking voice, and we
  sense and see the embarrassment of her children. But, then, her
  deep feeling comes across and the song takes effect as the scene
  ends.)*

MRS. JACKBURN *(Singing)*:
>   "Go down, Moses,
>   Way down in Egypt's land.
>   Tell old Pharaoh,
>   To let my people go . . ."

COMMENTATOR:
  Thank you very much, Mrs. Jackburn, and, also, Samuel and Bella
  Jackburn for your appearance on this program. *(Samuel and Bella
  try to smile as the commentator is handed a piece of paper. They
  go off lecturing their mother.)* We have a final, surprising piece
  of information in regard to Jackburn's ship. For this late development, we take you to the London airport.

14 (on film)

AIRPORT COMMENTATOR:
  I am standing here beside the private plane of Frank Terry, the
  American oil magnate. For several years, Mr. Terry has been running his vast European and Middle-East enterprises from his lovely
  eighteenth century estate, *Downeyglade,* in Surrey. May I ask
  where you're going today, Mr. Terry?

TERRY:
  We're just taking a little survey flight across the Alps. I'm planning

to run a pipe line from Northern Italy to Southern Germany
Should help quite a bit in the delivery of oil to the European
community.

COMMENTATOR:

What is your interest in Jackburn's ship?

TERRY:

Well, it's not so unusual. The public knows that for years I've been
supporting the Maritime Museum in Massachusetts. We've got
some of the most famous ships in the history of seafaring there

COMMENTATOR:

Have you made a definite offer for Jackburn's ship?

TERRY:

Well, it's a bit early to say that. After all, he's still holed up there
in the House. But it's fair to say I'm interested.

COMMENTATOR:

Could you tell us why, please?

TERRY:

Voyage, search, that's what counts in life. Now of course Jackburn
didn't sail his ship up the Thames. Evidently he just assembled it
in London for the supposed purpose of a civil rights demonstration
Still he plans to sail it to other ports . . .

COMMENTATOR:

What about the purpose of his voyage? Does he mean to use violence
if necessary?

TERRY:

We aren't sure of that yet. Anyway, it's the fact of a voyage that
counts in life. Nothing risked, nothing gained. There wouldn't be
any society without that motto.

COMMENTATOR *(Still probing)*:

But the fact that he invaded the House . . .

TERRY *(It's impossible to throw him off balance.)*:

Well, I have great respect for the House of Commons. Some of my
best friends are members of the House. It's a great institution
You can't damage it with a little adventure like Jackburn's ship.

COMMENTATOR *(A little subdued by Terry)*:

I dare say not . . . Thank you, Mr. Terry. *(To the audience)* We've been talking at the London Airport to Mr. Frank Terry, the American oil magnate, and that ends our special program on *The Black President.*

15

(The flag is drawn up on stage, revealing the Tea Room of the House again. It is late at night. Some cots have been set up. An argument is raging between Hooper, Peter, and a British naval officer. In the background, Jackburn is talking to the Nigerian and the West Indian.)

PETER:

How can we sleep here?

NAVAL OFFICER:

I'm sorry we haven't been able yet to arrange for your release.

HOOPER:

You're *negotiating* with him?

NAVAL OFFICER:

We don't want anyone to be injured, even by accident.

HOOPER:

But you want the British Navy to submit!

NAVAL OFFICER *(Stiffly)*:

That's hardly fair, Sir. We are in the House of Commons. At sea, I assure you, it would be quite a different story.

PETER:

I'm not worried about the British Navy. What about my wife? Have you notified the American Embassy?

NAVAL OFFICER *(Wearily)*:

I assure you she's in no danger. The American Embassy is fully aware of the problem. Jackburn has promised me that his demonstration is intended to be peaceful . . .
(They continue arguing.)

161

16

JACKBURN *(From the rear of the stage, observing)*:

Arguing, arguing. That's the danger of any kind of action. Every-body has to explain. Look at them.

WEST INDIAN:

I wish we'd been along when you raised the flag. You didn't have any trouble?

JACKBURN:

A few shouts about desecrating the House! After they saw that we intended only to raise the flag, the protests died out pretty much.

NIGERIAN:

I don't think they appreciate being the first Port of Honor.

WEST INDIAN:

Do you think they'll let us really sail?

JACKBURN:

We must sail. I've asked for a conference tomorrow with the Prime Minister.

WEST INDIAN *(Laughing)*:

The Prime Minister! I'd like to have seen their faces when you asked that.

17

(The spotlight moves over to where Carla, Johnny, and Fanny are talking.)

JOHNNY *(Disconsolately)*:

I had a date tonight too.

FANNY:

She'll read about you in the papers. Then she'll really want to go out with you.

JOHNNY:

Who's going to read about me? The papers will write about them *(pointing to Peter and Laura)*, VISITING YANKS TRAPPED IN HOUSE. Or *(pointing to Hooper)* him, RETIRED BRIT-ISH BUSINESS MAN, or whatever he is.

FANNY:

Why? We're sitting on something big. Nothing like this has happened in the House since Guy Fawkes tried to sneak in. The three of us could sell one of those eyewitness stories when it's over.

CARLA:

I don't like to make money out of this.

FANNY:

Why not?

CARLA:

Please, I do not understand what they do, but I think they try to do something for their people.

FANNY:

Hey, you turning black?

CARLA:

I am not stopping you. I just don't want to help.

FANNY (Disgusted):

How do you like that? So let's you and I talk, Johnny . . .

(She pulls Johnny away, leaving Carla alone. The spotlight shifts to Laura and Miss Hooper, where they are preparing for bed. Miss Hooper is in her element, for she is always at her best in semi-Spartan situations.)

18

MISS HOOPER (Helping Laura to fix the bed):

Let me show you how to do that, my dear. We learned all about those things during the war.

LAURA:

Thanks, I'm sorry to be jittery. As a child, we had Negro servants. They were nice, but distant. They used to play with me. That was the only level on which you could know a Negro, a child playing with them, like a game in the dark, darker, darker, until suddenly the game became dangerous.

MISS HOOPER:

Dangerous?

LAURA:

When you were older you were supposed to forget about Negroes as if they didn't exist.

MISS HOOPER:

I know, we have our own racial problems here in London.

LAURA:

It's not the same. To you the Negro's a foreigner. Every time I open a newspaper and see a picture of a mob jeering at some Negro student on his way to school, I see part of myself in those faces of hate.

MISS HOOPER:

With a little sleep, you'll feel better.

LAURA *(Wryly)*:

I'm afraid I won't sleep much. They look like Army cots. My husband was in the Army. I followed him from camp to camp. We lived in fifteen different towns.

MISS HOOPER:

Then you know what waiting is like.

LAURA *(Nervously)*:

I never got used to it.

MISS HOOPER:

It's funny, I had almost forgotten what it was like during the war. We waited every night for something to happen. The sirens began and ended everything. You had a strange sense of anticipation. Something was going to happen. We hated the war, but it was a change. We learned to live for each day.

(There is a flash of light and the reflection of flames from the direction of the ship on the river.)

LAURA *(Screaming out)*:

Fire! The ship's on fire!
(Everyone rushes to the window to look out. Offstage, the crew is heard singing, "Where's that ship gonna sail? etc.")

164

19

JACKBURN:

Please, ladies and gentlemen. It is only a celebration . . .

NAVAL OFFICER *(Angrily)*:

Captain Jackburn, you didn't say anything about this!

JACKBURN:

Must I mention all celebrations?

NAVAL OFFICER:

They're likely to burn down London!

JACKBURN *(Smiling)*:

It's only a little bonfire on deck. They sing a few songs. They may dance. We plan to do this at every Port of Honor to show joy, good will. When we establish better relations, we will invite people to be our guests, to sing and dance themselves.

NAVAL OFFICER *(Suspiciously)*:

What are they celebrating?

JACKBURN:

Our first raising of the flag.

'NAVAL OFFICER *(Bitterly)*:

Is that what you call a victory?

JACKBURN:

A celebration, not a victory.

NAVAL OFFICER *(Snapping)*:

Your celebration may be short. Until tomorrow morning . . .

JACKBURN:

I will be glad to see the Prime Minister.

NAVAL OFFICER:

You may not see anyone!

(Jackburn laughs, as the Naval Officer exits indignantly. The song is heard offstage, rising in intensity. The spotlight shifts to Peter and Laura.)

20

PETER:

Why doesn't the British government do something? They could free us in a moment.

LAURA:

If you were a government head, and a slave ship with a crew of Negroes sailed up to your headquarters to make a protest, would you sink them on the spot?

PETER:

At least I'd do something!

LAURA:

What?

PETER:

I don't know . . .

LAURA:

Peter, what do you really think of this Jackburn?

PETER:

He's crazy.

LAURA:

What's the opposite of crazy? Practical? Dull?

PETER:

Go to sleep. Don't romanticize him just because he's a Negro.

LAURA:

We've never talked much about Negroes.

PETER:

We've never seen them much in our town.

LAURA:

Because we hide them, a game of hide-and-don't-go-seek . . . In Europe everything looks so different. At home, we think we're such a peaceful country, but here . . .

(She sings)

When Europe sees America,
It sees our land

Running with blood,
A racial flood;
A sea of white and black violence
Flowing into silence . . .

(After a pause) That's not a pleasant view of our country . . .

PETER *(Shortly)*:
It's only part true . . .

21

HOOPER *(Annoyed at his sister's expert camping)*:
Don't try to make me comfortable!

MISS HOOPER:
There's no harm in being cosy.

HOOPER:
I must say you treat this rather like a camping expedition of Girl Guides.

MISS HOOPER:
It isn't every day one gets a chance to sleep in the Commons.

HOOPER *(Snorting)*:
Nonsense!

MISS HOOPER:
Do you want me to sleep on a bed of spikes? I want to meet all of the famous ghosts here in my dreams.

HOOPER:
You won't need to dream, just close your eyes. In this country it's easier to live in the past than the present.

(They sing, "For England Is Ruled By Its Past.")

MISS HOOPER *(Singing)*:
What a chance!
To camp in the House of Commons!
To meet the ghosts of Gladstone,
Disraeli, and Lloyd George!
If I'm to meet those ministers of mystery

167

In their place of history,
I want to be prepared to shake their hand.

HOOPER *(Sings)*:

For England is ruled by its past.
We don't care much about the future.
When you have a past that's grand,
You can never live it down.
You learn that all the hosts
Who summon you are famous ghosts.
You learn to live within the past.

THE HOOPERS *(Together)*:

For England is ruled by its past.
We don't care much about the future.
When you learn that all the hosts
Who summon you are famous ghosts,
You learn to live within the past.

22

(The lighting changes as the song of the crew offstage is heard softly in the distance. Jackburn is asleep. The Nigerian is on guard. Hesitantly, Carla approaches.)

CARLA:

Please, I would like to talk to Mr. Jackburn.

JACKBURN *(Waking up)*:

Who is it?

NIGERIAN:

The Spanish girl.

JACKBURN *(Coming forward)*:

What do you want?

CARLA:

When you ask where I come from, I say Spain. You say, "Spain, that's different." You are going to sail your ship to Spain?

JACKBURN *(Laughing)*:

You think I'm a madman trying to free the world?

CARLA:

I do not know what to think. Where did you get the idea of your ship?

JACKBURN *(Ironically)*:

Back in *the* war.

CARLA:

Which war?

JACKBURN:

The war, World War II, *the* war against fascism, *the* war for racial equality, *the* war for the defense of democracy.

CARLA:

I was a child then. I knew only stories of our Civil War, when my father spent a year in prison because he sympathized with the Republicans against Franco. One day, after the world war is over, I am twelve, Franco opens a huge war memorial. My father takes me there. We wander through it with many other silent people. No one says a word. Endless space filled in with marble. Long, cold halls and statues. Everything is large, so large and dead, like the things you see in a nightmare.

JACKBURN:

Everyone has his own war to remember. Mine was in the American Army, Fort Warren, Wyoming. You know where that is in the West?

CARLA *(Smiling)*:

I have only seen the West in films.

JACKBURN:

That's the only place it exists any more. Fort Warren was an old Army post with big, wooden buildings full of rooms, where officers brought up large families in the old days, six, seven children.

CARLA:

Were they Catholic officers?

JACKBURN *(Smiling)*:

No, just family officers. Plenty of lazy time in those days. You herded cattle in your backyard. The officers had plenty of time to breed.

169

CARLA:
Breed?

JACKBURN:
Make children.

CARLA *(Blushing)*:
Oh.

JACKBURN:
It wasn't that kind of life by World War II. Then it was a Quarter-master Training Center.

(FILM BACKGROUND: As Jackburn talks, the screen behind him lights up with a silent film. Shots of the Quartermaster Training Center at Fort Warren.)

CARLA:
I don't understand.

JACKBURN:
The Quartermaster supplies the Army. They do all the dirty work feeding, clothing. That's where most of the colored men were stuck I arrived in Fort Warren with 250 other blacks from the South I was ashamed of them. I was ashamed of myself.

(FILM BACKGROUND: Shots of soldiers working and drilling on the post. The camera moves in to show that most of them are black Then we see the arrival of large groups of Negro soldiers from the South. As the camera reveals their faces, it is apparent that they are totally disinterested in Army service.)

CARLA:
Why?

JACKBURN:
Some of the Southern draft boards saw an easy way of getting rid of their worst blacks and keeping white boys at home. So they put their undesirable blacks in the Army and shipped them off to Fort Warren. Most of them had to be discharged fast. You're not much good as a soldier when you have an advanced case of syphilis.

CARLA:

Many had syphilis?

(FILM BACKGROUND: *Shots of a transient Negro company falling out for sick call. Jackburn is seen calling the roll. Then he is seen marching the soldiers to the hospital.*)

JACKBURN:

In our company there were over a hundred cases of venereal disease, gonorrhea and syphilis. Every Monday night was sick call. I called the roll. *Adams, Anderson, Cobb, Davis* ... I can still remember all the names. I can recite the whole roll call in my sleep. After calling the roll, the white duty officer marched us over to the hospital. As they went in for their shots, I checked off their names. One Monday I slipped into line and got a shot too. I don't know why ... Afterwards they were all laughing at me ... "Jackburn, he got a shot too!" ... "How's the syph, Jackburn?" ...

CARLA:

Please, I don't like this story ...

JACKBURN *(Savagely)*:

You wanted to find out about me ... *(Then, he continues more calmly.)* We didn't get much time off at Fort Warren. The officers didn't want us to go into town. The town was afraid of colored men. Why not, with the reputation we had? We hated the town because in the few hours we were allowed there on pass, nothing would open to us except a couple of locked doors if you had money ...

(FILM BACKGROUND: *Shots of an alley in the city, run-down wooden buildings. Jackburn is seen walking up the alley. He climbs the steps of one of the buildings and knocks on the door. No answer. He pounds violently on the door. Slowly, the door opens and he disappears inside.*)

One evening I came out of one of those locked doors dead drunk. The hell with time! All those stars up in the sky, weaving around ... I staggered into the Fort. Everyone was lined up on the parade grounds for retreat — when they blow taps and salute the flag to end the day.

171

(FILM BACKGROUND: *Jackburn staggers out of the building. Quick distorted shots of the sky, the alley, the road, images of his drunken vision. Shots of the Negro troops lined up on the parade ground for retreat. Their rigid order is contrasted in alternating shots with Jackburn's whirling images of the Fort as he enters the military post.)*

When I saw all those black faces lined up in front of the white officers something broke. What a bunch of soldiers! I began to laugh, crazy laughter. I couldn't stop . . . I took off all my clothes. When I was naked, I strutted stiffly up to our company commander and saluted him. I was giving the whole damn business a salute, the Army, the country, the war, the whole works. Here's a salute for you and you and you!

(FILM BACKGROUND: *Shots of Jackburn breaking into crazy laughter contrasted with shots of the soldiers at rigid attention becoming increasingly uneasy. Suddenly Jackburn is taking off his clothes. Naked, he salutes the company commander. The camera moves in on a close-up of the commander's astonished, gaping face.)*

(On stage, Carla is moved. Jackburn pauses a moment, looking at her, before he continues in a more quiet tone.)

A couple of white officers grabbed me and rushed me off. Some soldiers thought one of the white officers kicked me. I don't remember I was so drunk . . . I was struggling and laughing, laughing at the salute. They were pushing me along . . . Suddenly, all the colored troops broke ranks and rushed for those white officers. They dropped me and ran for the Headquarters building. They barely made it and locked the door. Then the soldiers went crazy. They broke into the supply room and kitchen and stole guns and food. Finally, riot troops were called out. They had to use tear gas and even a tank. Two blacks, who became leaders of the riot, were killed. They locked themselves in a room and wouldn't give up. Men full of hate, bitterness, violent men who had served time in jail for knifing and robbery . . . Suddenly, in that riot, they became leaders.

(FILM BACKGROUND: *Shots from above of the colored troops breaking ranks. Jackburn is seen struggling and laughing as the white*

172

*officers push him along. The officers drop Jackburn and run for
the Headquarters building as the troops chase them. The two
blacks, leaders of the riot, are shown directing the entry into the
supply room and the kitchen. Quick shots of the riot troops with
their gas masks and the tank. Under the impact of the tear gas,
the rioters scatter and retreat. Shots of the two black leaders barricaded in the room, the tank moving towards them.)*

ARLA :
What happened to you?

ACKBURN :
I was court-martialed and given a year in prison. Since I was drunk
and didn't have syphilis and was more educated than the rest, they
were lenient with me. I served only a few months in the Guard
House, walking around in green fatigue clothes with a huge, white
P for Prisoner painted on my back. After I served my time, I was
discharged from the Army. Psychologically unfit for military
service. You know something? There was never a hint of that
riot in the newspapers. No one except people who were there on
the post ever heard that two blacks were killed and several hundred
colored troops arrested. And I started it all . . .

(FILM BACKGROUND: *Lonely shots of Jackburn collecting and
emptying garbage cans, the huge "P" prominently painted on his
green fatigues. A lazy, bored guard with a shotgun is following
him. Then Jackburn is seen before the Discharge Board as they
examine him critically. As the film sequence ends, Jackburn is
taking off his uniform and putting on civilian clothes, contemplating
the difference between the uniform and the suit.)*

ARLA :
I'm glad you told me. I had bad beginning in Spain too. A bad beginning is not always the end.

ACKBURN *(Smiling a little):*
What do you do if a beginning is bad?
(They sing "What Can You Do If A Beginning Is Bad?")

ARLA :

Spain is a memory of freedom
That I'm too young to know,

173

A beginning that went bad,
A spring that turned to snow.

JACKBURN:

What can you do if a beginning is bad,
But work for an ending that's good?
You can't live under the shadow
Of the executioner's hood . . .

I live in a memory of freedom
That I'm too old to have known,
A beginning that went bad,
A harvest never sown.

CARLA:

What can you do if a beginning is bad,
But work for the ending that's good?

TOGETHER:

What can you do if a beginning is bad?
You work for the ending that's good.

JACKBURN *(As the song from the ship is heard, louder again):*
Listen to 'em . . . How would you like to see the ship? You'll be ou
first visitor!

CARLA:
I don't think I . . .

JACKBURN *(Grinning):*
Come on. Captain Moses Jackburn says it's all right.

CARLA *(Smiling):*
I would like to see your ship.

JACKBURN *(Warning her):*
Don't expect too much. It's only a small, cramped ship that hasn'
sailed anywhere yet. It has to sail a long way if it's going to d
any good.

(Members of the crew have been appearing on stage.)

174

THE CREW *(Singing)*:

> Where's that ship gonna sail?
> Sail here, sail there, sail everywhere.
> Jackburn sail, Jackburn free,
> Jackburn got that freedom ship.
> Sail man, sail, sail everywhere.

JACKBURN *and* CARLA *(Singing)*:

> What can you do if a beginning is bad?
> You work for the ending that's good.

(Then, with the crew)

> Where's that ship gonna sail?
> Sail, man, sail that *Black President.*
> Sail here, sail there, sail everywhere.

(They all begin to dance and sing)

> Where's that ship gonna sail?
> Sail here, sail there, sail everywhere.
> Jackburn sail, Jackburn free,
> Jackburn sail that freedom ship.
> Sail man, sail, sail everywhere!

(The crew serenade Jackburn and Carla as he takes her off to the ship, and the curtain falls on Part I.)

INTERMISSION

PART II

1

(The flag is down and Part II begins with a film sequence. The television commentator, either on stage or on film, introduces the sequence.)

COMMENTATOR:

We take you now to a roadside gas station in Georgia, where our traveling BBC correspondent has been covering the latest development in connection with Jackburn's ship.

(A small, dusty gas station in Georgia is seen. Several figures in white pointed hoods and long white robes are standing around a table covered with leaflets. A large sign reads, FREE COFFEE. A motorist enters the station.)

FIRST KLANSMAN *(Politely)*:
Cream and sugar on the table over there, Sir.

SECOND KLANSMAN:
Some good reading for you.

THIRD KLANSMAN *(Giving the motorist some leaflets)*:
You might like to study these documents, Sir.

MOTORIST:
I thought you fellows were declared illegal.

FIRST KLANSMAN:
Oh no, Sir, you're confusing us with the Ku Klux Klan. We're the Four K's, the Knights of the Ku Klux Klan, Incorporated. We're completely different.

MOTORIST:
I see . . . *(Reading from a leaflet)* "Since some Negro ministers, politicians, and some white people are so anxious to 'mix socially,' or sometimes known as integrate, let us White People who want to stay in the White Race wake up and think." Are you people against the Negroes?

FIRST KLANSMAN:
Not *against,* Sir, that's a strong word. We don't like the old way of handling things. Nigg . . . I mean Negroes are all right if they stick to their own way of life.

SECOND KLANSMAN *(Confidentially)*:
But the Negro really wants the privilege of marrying a white lady.

THIRD KLANSMAN:
You see, Sir, we feel that we don't have to submit to all these sit-ins and all the other push-in movements by the Negro.

MOTORIST:
What are you going to do?

FIRST KLANSMAN:
Organize all over the world, try to awaken the white race.

176

MOTORIST:
Even in Europe?

FIRST KLANSMAN:
In England too. We have friends there and we're trying to help
them stop such disgraceful raids as this *Black President.*

MOTORIST:
Say, didn't this Negro, Jackburn, come from Georgia?

SECOND KLANSMAN:
Maybe he did, but not for long. We got rid of him.
(The Klansmen sing)

KLANSMEN:

> Black is black
> And white is white
> And never the twain shall meet.
> Walking down the street,
> You don't want darky-ness,
> You want a skin of white.
> Under the moon
> And under the sun
> We'll sing this tune:
> Black is black
> And white is white
> And never the twain shall meet.

MOTORIST *(Casually, after the song):*
What about lynching?

FIRST KLANSMAN *(Smiling thinly):*
Sir, that is not funny. You're thinking of the old Klan.

SECOND KLANSMAN *(More meancingly):*
You're not from the North are you?

MOTORIST *(Hastily):*
No, I'm from England.

THIRD KLANSMAN *(Relaxing):*
In that case you're welcome. Have some more coffee.

SECOND KLANSMAN *(Giving him more pamphlets)*:
Have some more pamphlets.

FIRST KLANSMAN:
We're sorry you English have to be bothered with this Jackburn. I hope you send him to jail.

(A young tough in jeans and leather jacket slouches up to the Motorist.)

YOUNG TOUGH:
Hey, dad ... Can I talk to you a minute? *(He draws the Motorist aside.)* Look, you want some action?

MOTORIST *(Bewildered)*:
I don't understand.

YOUNG TOUGH *(Gesturing scornfully at the Klansmen)*:
It takes more than a bunch of old dames in some sheets passing out propaganda ... Where you come from?

MOTORIST:
England.

YOUNG TOUGH:
My relatives came from England ... *(Then, with a grin)* Long time ago. You come to Woolworths tomorrow at noon, you'll see some real action.

MOTORIST:
What are you going to do?

YOUNG TOUGH:
We take care of these sit-down boys. These Niggers think they know so much, puttin' on this educated act. They bring along books, we knock 'em out of their hands. We push 'em around a bit. Come see for yourself, dad. *(He waves and exits.)*

MOTORIST *(He takes a small microphone from his pocket and turns to the audience, as the Klansmen behind him are singing and passing out leaflets and coffee.)*:
That's all for today from your BBC correspondent touring the American South ...

178

2

*The flag is drawn up to reveal the Tea Room again. Jackburn is gazing
out the window at his ship. The others are sitting, resting, or waiting
disconsolately, some playing cards, most of them doing nothing. The
West Indian moves excitedly from the door to tell Jackburn of a visitor.
The visitor, in a diplomat's formal, conservative suit, is seen entering
into a spotlit area upstage, as if it were a small, private room.)*

WEST INDIAN *(Grinning)*:

That Naval Officer's back, Captain. He don't look very happy. I
don't think England is a happy country.

*(The Naval Officer enters and stops stiffly before Jackburn. It is
obvious that the Naval Officer is on an unwelcome mission.)*

NAVAL OFFICER *(Stiffly)*:

Mr. Jackburn ...

JACKBURN *(Correcting him genially)*:

Captain Jackburn.

NAVAL OFFICER *(Acidly)*:

Captain Jackburn, a representative of the government will see you.

JACKBURN *(Baiting him)*:

The Prime Minister?

NAVAL OFFICER *(Haughtily)*:

There was never any question of the Prime Minister. Lord Manning
will see you.

JACKBURN:

Lord who?

NAVAL OFFICER:

Lord Manning is in the Foreign Office. You are to understand this
meeting is completely confidential. If you ever mention this meeting
with his Lordship, the government will deny that such a meeting
has taken place.

JACKBURN *(Ironically)*:

Has the agenda for our talk been printed and the properly shaped
table prepared?

NAVAL OFFICER *(Stiffly)*:

  I trust that you will appreciate the serious desire of our government for a peaceful conclusion to your adventure without unnecessary violence.

JACKBURN *(Grandly)*:

  Please convey me to the honorable Lord and I will do my best to cooperate with his Lordship and avoid undue violence.

  (The Naval Officer glares at him. Jackburn follows him out to the lighted area on the forestage where Lord Manning is waiting. The back of the stage is darkened. The Naval Officer withdraws as Lord Manning greets Jackburn.)

3

LORD MANNING:

  Captain Jackburn, the conditions of this meeting were explained to you?

JACKBURN:

  If I divulge a word of our conference, Her Majesty's Government will deny that such a meeting took place.

LORD MANNING:

  That is correct. *(Then, smiling)* It sounds absurd, doesn't it?

JACKBURN *(Grinning)*:

  I'm afraid I seem a little absurd too.

LORD MANNING *(They laugh)*:

  Shall we sit down? *(He motions to two chairs and they sit.)* With two people, we have the advantage that it's impossible to sit around a round table. Every time I walk into a conference room, I see a round table offering supposedly equal status with everyone's name on identical signs with letters exactly the same size. In my own house, I'm afraid, I have a passion for rectangular tables.

JACKBURN *(Softly)*:

  What does Her Majesty's government want?

LORD MANNING *(With a sigh)*:

  So we're to be direct with each other then. I suspected as much. I will allow myself to be interrogated first if you wish.

JACKBURN *(Shrugging)*:

It's up to you how long you want to beat around the bush. I'm no philosopher. I'm just black.

LORD MANNING:

Black eliminates philosophy in favor of action. Is that what you mean?

JACKBURN:

I mean black is tired of being fenced around with arguments.

LORD MANNING:

Your ship is not an argument?

JACKBURN:

It's an action, I hope. *(Then, grinning)* At least the imitation of an action.

LORD MANNING:

I didn't question your education. I am interested in your action. Who paid for it?

JACKBURN:

I don't mind telling you. Mostly blacks who are tired of waiting. They wanted to do something and they liked my idea of a slave ship. It didn't cost much to build. You see, already we've shifted the subject from you to me.

LORD MANNING *(Reflecting)*:

I seem to have developed a habit of doing that more and more recently. In these international conferences one learns to cultivate the talent of anonymous evasion. The bone of a plan is tossed upon a conference table and everyone begins to worry it in the name of progress.

(He sings, with Jackburn, "Progress is a Bone")

> Progress is a bone
> Tossed on the top
> Of a conference table
> To rest there like a stone.
> You worry it
> And it remains the same.
> Progress is a bone.

JACKBURN *(Singing in reply):*

> Progress is a black bone
> Tossed on the top
> Of a white conference table
> To rest there alone.
> You worry it
> And it begins to move.
> Progress is a rolling stone.

LORD MANNING:
Let it roll ... It remains a bone ...

TOGETHER:

JACKBURN:	LORD MANNING:
Progress is a black bone,	Progress is a bone ...
Moving, moving	It remains a bone ...
In its black skin!	It cannot move ...
Rolling through the world,	It remains a stone.
Progress is a rolling stone.	

(After the song, Jackburn extends his hand abruptly to Lord Manning.)

JACKBURN:
Shake hand with black skin and bones. We haven't done that yet.

(They shake hands. Jackburn grips Lord Manning's hand tightly.)

That's a black hand you're shaking ...

LORD MANNING *(Slowly):*
It doesn't feel any different than a white hand.

JACKBURN *(Still holding Lord Manning's hand tightly):*
You think that hand wants nothing better than to be white. You're
wrong. That hand doesn't go around like a slave any more. That
hand knows black is a beautiful color. Beautiful because it's learned
to be feared. There's an old slave song yearning for heaven —
(he sings) "I know my robe's going to fit me well. I tried it on
at the gates of Hell." Watch out when that black hand tries to
climb up into your white heaven! *(Finally, he releases Lord Manning's hand.)*

LORD MANNING *(Flexing his hand a little ruefully):*
I see what you mean . . . I wonder if the color black will be as exclusive in heaven as the color white has been.

JACKBURN :
That's up to you and your kind.

LORD MANNING :
I'm afraid the matter is more complex . . . I must inform you of some precautions Her Majesty's Government has taken in council with other western governments. If you ever try to sail your ship into international waters, it will be stopped by appropriate vessels, searched for evidence of piracy, and sunk as a menace to navigation and peace on the high seas.

JACKBURN *(Staring at Lord Manning):*
Did your "council" include any black diplomats?

LORD MANNING :
It did.

JACKBURN :
What happens to my crew?

LORD MANNING :
That depends on you.

JACKBURN :
You got that old bone all figured out.

LORD MANNING :
If you are willing to give up your ship peacefully, it is all likely to be treated as a romantic adventure.

JACKBURN *(Bitterly):*
Do I keep the film rights?

LORD MANNING :
Don't misunderstand me. We are perfectly aware of the change in power. When I say progress is a bone, I am only stating my own belief that human nature does not change. Man's primitive, racial fears remain concealed under the shifting social laws. The law has come to believe in black equality, and we believe in the law.

If you act peacefully now, you can even sell your ship to any buyer you wish. I will be waiting for your wise decision. Goodbye and good luck, Captain Jackburn. *(He exits.)*

JACKBURN *(Staring after him):*
A romantic adventure... Is that all it's been?
(He shakes his head and sings wistfully):

> Progress is a black bone
> Tossed on the top
> Of a white conference table
> To rest there alone... alone... alone...

(The "alone" echoes as an isolated refrain. Then, with growing defiance and bitter emotion):

> You worry it
> And it begins to move,
> Progress is a rolling, black stone.

(At the end of the scene, he is sitting, reflecting. He stays there throughout the next film sequence as the screen lights up.)

4

(Film sequence: The trial of Nelson Mandela in Pretoria, South Africa, April, 1964. Mandela is seen in the court, rising and stepping into the witness-box to explain his acts. His actual speech was four and a half hours long. The court sentenced him to life imprisonment.)

MANDELA:
I am the first accused. My name is Nelson Mandela. I hold a Bachelor's Degree in Arts and practiced as an attorney in Johannesburg for a number of years in partnership with Oliver Tambo. I am a convincted prisoner serving five years for leaving the country without a permit and for inciting people to go on strike at the end of May, 1961. At the outset I want to say that the suggestion made by the State in its opening that the struggle in South Africa is under the

influence of foreigners or Communists is wholly incorrect. I have done whatever I did, both as an individual and as a leader of my people, because of my experience in South Africa and my own proudly felt African background.

In my youth in the Transkei I listened to the elders of my tribe telling stories of the old days. Among the tales they related to me were those of wars fought by our ancestors in defense of the fatherland. The names of Dingane and Bambata, Hintsa and Makana, Squngthi and Dalasile, Moshoeshoe and Sekhukhuni were praised as the glory of the entire African nation. I hoped then that life might offer me the opportunity to serve my people and make my own humble contribution to their freedom struggle. This is what has motivated me in all that I have done.

Some of the things told so far to the court are true and some are untrue. I do not, however, deny that I planned sabotage. I did not plan it in a spirit of recklessness, nor because I have any love of violence. I planned it as a result of a calm and sober assessment of the political situation that had arisen after many years of tyranny, exploitation and oppression of my people by the whites . . .

At the beginning of June, 1961, after a long and anxious assessment of the South African situation, I, and some colleagues, came to the conclusion that as violence in this country was inevitable, it would be unrealistic and wrong for African leaders to continue preaching peace and non-violence at a time when the Government met our peaceful demands with force.

Umkonto was formed in November, 1961. Umkonto was to perform sabotage, and strict instructions were given to its members right from the start that on no account were they to injure or kill people in planning or carrying out operations. The fight which held out the best prospect for us and the least risk of life to both sides was guerrilla warfare. I started to make a study of the art of war and revolution and, whilst abroad, underwent a course in military training. If there was to be guerrilla warefare, I wanted to be able to stand and fight with my people and to share the hazards of war with them . . .

I have always regarded myself as an African patriot. After all, I was born in Umtata 46 years ago. My guardian was my cousin, who was acting paramount chief of Tembuland, and I am related both to the present paramount chief of Tembuland, Sabata Dalinyebo, and to Kaizer Matanzima, the Chief Minister of the Transkei.

185

It is true, as I have already stated, that I have been influenced by Marxist thought. But this is also true of many of the leaders of the new independent States. Such widely different persons as Gandhi, Nehru, Nkrumah and Nasser all acknowledge this fact. We all accept the need for some form of Socialism to enable our people to catch up with the advanced countries of this world and to overcome their legacy of extreme poverty. But this does not mean we are Marxists . . .

I have great respect for British political institutions, and for the country's system of justice. I regard the British Parliament as the most democratic institution in the world, and the independence and impartiality of its judiciary never fail to arouse my admiration.

I have been influenced in my thinking by both West and East. All this has led me to feel that I should tie myself to no particular system of society other than of Socialism. I must leave myself free to borrow the best from the West and from the East.

Basically, we fight against two features which are the hallmarks of African life in South Africa and which are entrenched by legislation which we seek to have repealed. These features are poverty and the lack of human dignity.

South Africa is the richest country in Africa, and could be one of the richest countries in the world. But it is a land of extremes and remarkable contrasts. The whites enjoy what may well be the highest standard of living in the world, whilst Africans live in poverty and misery.

The lack of human dignity experienced by Africans is the direct result of the policy of white supremacy. White supremacy implies black inferiority. Legislation designed to preserve white supremacy entrenches this notion.

Africans want to be paid a living wage. Africans want to perform work which they are capable of doing, and not work which the Government declares them to be capable of. Africans want to be allowed to live where they obtain work, and not be forced out of an area because they were not born there. Africans want to be allowed to own land in places where they work, and not to be obliged to live in rented houses which they can never call their own. Africans want to be part of the general population, and not confined to living in their own ghettos. Above all, we want equal political rights because without them our disabilities will be permanent . . .

186

During my lifetime I have dedicated myself to this struggle of the African people. I have fought against white domination, and I have fought against black domination. I have cherished the ideal of a democratic and free society in which all persons live together in harmony and with equal opportunities. It is an ideal which I hope to live for and to see realized. But if needs be, my Lord, it is an ideal for which I am prepared to die.

5

(As the film fades out, the West Indian and the Nigerian enter and confront Jackburn, who is still sitting there, reflecting.)

NIGERIAN :

Are they going to let us sail?

JACKBURN :

After our ship reaches international waters, it will be stopped by quote—appropriate vessels—unquote, searched for evidence of piracy, and sunk as a menace to navigation and peace on the high seas. The Lord says if we act peacefully and give up the ship now, it'll all be treated as a romantic adventure ...

WEST INDIAN :

Romantic adventure?

JACKBURN :

You know, the age of romance is over, so put it in a newspaper or film; put all that romantic stuff on a great, big screen, like a dream without too much reality, and it can't hurt you.

NIGERIAN :

What happens to the heroes of this romantic adventure?

JACKBURN :

They all get sent back to their segregated homes.

WEST INDIAN :

And the ship?

JACKBURN:

We might sell it to Mr. Terry's Maritime Museum. The conquering
heroes return home with legendary halos and coins in their purse.

WEST INDIAN:

I don't like this romantic adventure. They don't cast any blacks in
Hollywood. I am not the ghost of Errol Flynn.

NIGERIAN:

If we sail, the ship will be sunk. We might even be tried for piracy in
a white court with a black judge as a token gesture if there's one
around.

JACKBURN:

That's the choice.

NIGERIAN *(Turning on Jackburn):*

Perhaps we were wrong when we agreed that Nationalism is impossible today.

JACKBURN:

You think a black world is possible?

NIGERIAN:

Not one big one, but a few small ones perhaps.

WEST INDIAN:

Let's call the men and decide. This is still a democratic army.

JACKBURN:

Call them, but I'm still the Captain.

NIGERIAN:

Act like a captain then. Do we always have to give in to the white
man?

JACKBURN *(Bitterly):*

What do you want? Use your H-bomb to blow up the white world?

WEST INDIAN:

Why quarrel? We don't have the H-bomb yet.

NIGERIAN *(To Jackburn):*

The choice is what we want. Isn't that what you told us? The time
has come to decide. Perhaps we have to give up your romantic

voyage and start in with black lives, get out of the white world. *(He sings):*

> What do blacks want out of life?
> Only white kings are crowned ...
> Shall we be cooks and chauffeurs
> Or clean up underground?

(The crew members have come out on stage.)

WEST INDIAN *(Singing ironically):*
> Some of us are smart enough to take tickets,
> Or move quick enough to serve drinks.
> We're plenty strong to lift the garbage,
> We're fine at cleaning up kitchen sinks.

JACKBURN *(Crying out):*
What can we do in a black world?

THE CREW *(A mime-dance, as they sing):*
> In a black world we can be
> captains and kings,
> In a black world we can be
> fliers with wings.
>
> In a black world we can be
> lion and claws,
> In a black world we can be
> judged by black laws.
>
> In a black world we can see
> black clouds of grace,
> In a black world we can see
> God's big, black face.
>
> In a black world we can be
> Free! Free in a black world!

JACKBURN *(Speaking to them passionately):*
You think you can tear down all those little signs *White Ladies and Colored Women* by just making a black world? So the White Man's Heaven is the Black Man's Hell ... Do you think the Black Man's Heaven is going to be the White Man's Hell? What can we do in a black world?

189

THE CREW *(Dance-mime again, as they sing)*:
> In a black world we can wear
> > black angels' wings,
> In a black world we can be
> > captains and kings.
>
> In a black world we can see
> > black is not night,
> In a black world we can see
> > white is not light.
>
> In a black world we can be
> > dancers and song,
> In a black world we can go
> > dreaming along.
>
> In a black world we can be
> Free! Free in a black world!

(They freeze as the screen lights up and the next sequence is on film.)

6

(A Muslim street corner rally in New York or Chicago is shown on film. Shots of grim housing units and a drab street. Then, the camera moves in on a sound truck with a Negro standing on top of it talking to a few, scattered Negroes listening on the corner. The speaker is dressed entirely in black.)

SPEAKER *(Passionately, with great conviction)*:
The white god is an invention of the white man to keep the black man in line. They speak at us, through us, into us, around us, but we're the only ones who can speak for ourselves. That's why we support Elijah Muhammed, who represents the black man's lost past. Under his leadership, we've given up looking into the mirror and saying, "Boy, am I ugly." Now we look into that mirror and say, "Behold a black man."

Up to now we've been fed white, white, white. White is clean, black is dirty. White lives high on the green hills of God, black lives in the

Devil's slums. White is intelligence, black is ignorance. But where have archaeologists discovered the bones of the first man? In Tanganyika! And where have they discovered the bones of the second man? In the Union of South Africa! *(Laughter and delight among the listeners)* So not only the first man was black, but the second one too! *(More delight and laughter.)*

That's why Elijah Muhammed says God is black! All black men belong to Islam. You've been chosen to survive the war of Armageddon when the white man will wipe himself out! We want no part of their white wars! Why should we keep on suffering under the so-called name of Negro, when it is the will of Allah that this lost, black nation be returned to the true faith which is Islam.

Allah, through his good will, allowed the Devil to carry on infernal, scientific experiments which resulted in the creation of the white man, and, even worse, the creation of the white woman. *(More grins and chuckles among the listeners)* And Allah decreed that the white devils would rule the world for a certain length of time. Now Allah, through Elijah Muhammed, wants to restore the rule of peace that the white devils destroyed! *(Camera on a spectator applauding enthusiastically.)*

Even the Jew nowadays has a nation and a flag. "Return to your true religion," Elijah has written. "Throw off the chains of the white slavemaster, the devil, and return to the fold. Stop drinking his alcohol, using his dope, protect your women, and forsake the filthy swine!"

Look in that mirror and see black is the most beautiful color in the world. Black is the color for that lovely God, Allah, and his minister, Elijah Muhammed!

(The camera moves in on the speaker's exultant face as he finishes his talk.)

7

(As the screen image fades out after 6, Jackburn turns to the crew.)

JACKBURN:

Maybe our ship *The Black President* was a crazy idea...

WEST INDIAN:
It's not so crazy.

NIGERIAN:
It's only crazy about Nationalism. *(A pause)*

JACKBURN *(Looking at the crew):*
That's where you think I went wrong?

WEST INDIAN:
What can you do against nations unless you're a nation yourself?
We're a pretty funny nation...

(They look at each other and begin to laugh.)

THE CREW, JACKBURN, NIGERIAN and WEST INDIAN *(As they sing, they dance and mime the satirical action of "We're a Pretty Funny Nation.")*:

> We're a pretty funny nation
> With a little boat for salvation;
> We're no Polaris missile.
> Our little ship's a tiny whistle
>   in the noisy world.
> If you want to rule today,
> You've got to sound off with a BANG!
>
> We're a pretty funny nation
> With a little boat for salvation;
> We thought we'd sail, sail,
> But if you're small, you're gonna fail, fail.
>
> Today, you've gotta be big,
> You've gotta be big enough to dig
> Way down underground so far
> That you can shoot way up to any star.
> You've gotta be moon-struck;
> You've gotta hit that piece of cheese
> Way up there in the midnight sky,
> Or else you're gonna die.
> Today, you've gotta be big.
> There's no future for you
> If you can't be a red-hot nation

192

With your radiation.
You've gotta have the highest brass,
You can't sit on your ass.
You've gotta have armies and navies,
Officers and politicians,
Big lawyers,   and THINGS,
You've gotta have lots of THINGS
If you want salvation as a nation.

Today, you've gotta be big.
You've gotta have THE BOMB
And sound off with a BANG!
You've gotta have that old detergent . . .
        You mean, DETERRENT!
        that old, deodorized, clean bomb,
        (not any *dirty* bomb),
Today, you've gotta be BIG
If you want salvation as a nation.

(After the ensemble number, the West Indian turns to Jackburn.)

WEST INDIAN:
  What happens to the ship?

JACKBURN *(Bitterly)*:
  You all want to give it up. I'll call Terry.

WEST INDIAN:
  You crazy, man?

NIGERIAN:
  Then what we got left?

JACKBURN:
  A big monument to the age of romance . . .

CREW MEMBERS *(Reacting pro and con)*:
  Don't sell the ship! Why not? We gotta get home. Who wants a
  damn monument? Don't sell the ship! etc . . .

JACKBURN:
  You got anything else in mind? *(An uncomfortable silence)* Go on,
  leave me alone . . .

193

(The crew members exit except for the Nigerian and the West India
who remain on stage in the shadows during Jackburn's talk with Terry.

8

(Terry appears on film in his home or office. His desk has various shi
models on it. A secretary hovers in the background. Jackburn is talkin
to him from a phone on stage.)

JACKBURN:

Hello, Mr. Terry. This is Moses Jackburn.

TERRY:

Yes . . .

JACKBURN:

You wanted to buy our ship, *The Black President* . . .

TERRY:

I'm glad you've decided to surrender.

JACKBURN:

I don't know about surrender . . . I'm giving it up, but my price ha
gone up a little.

TERRY:

I'm afraid I can't pay any more . . .

JACKBURN:

I don't mean just money. You're a connoisseur, Mr. Terry. You lik
good oil, good paintings, good food?

TERRY *(Stiffly)*:

My private life is not a subject for discussion.

JACKBURN:

You realize you're buying a black ship?

TERRY:

What are you talking about?

JACKBURN:

The Black President is a pitch-black ship. You can't hardly put it i
a white corner of your museum.

194

TERRY:

I don't understand . . .

JACKBURN:

If I sell you *The Black President,* I want you to put it in a black corner, maybe in the middle of a *barracoon.*

TERRY:

A what?

JACKBURN:

That's where the word *coon* comes from, Mr. Terry. A barracks for coons . . . That's what they called the slave stockades in Africa.

TERRY:

Are you crazy?

JACKBURN:

This is a real bargain. The idea is free. On top of the deck I want you to put up a screen for movies . . .

TERRY *(Dazed):*

Movies?

JACKBURN:

That way you can show the whole thing from start to finish. Begin in the barra-coons and show 'em herded on ship. The shipfitter, the old craftsman, chains 'em two by two at wrist and ankle. Then, they're thrust below into the stowage decks with maybe three feet clearance. Some of 'em lie side by side. Some sit up in each other's laps. You can show all that on film, maybe even hire a few, live, unemployed niggers to sit around in chains on the ship to show just what it was like.

TERRY *(Angrily):*

Jackburn, I don't like your saying niggers.

JACKBURN:

You've got to show *niggers,* Mr. Terry, if you're buying a black slave ship. I want you to show the real, black, heroic voyage in a real corner of your museum.

TERRY *(Outraged, beckoning frantically to the secretary who has been hovering like a butterfly in the blackground):*

Mine is a historical museum, Mr. Jackburn, not a publicity show! I'm interested in culture, a museum is culture! I want to give the youngsters today a feeling of the great maritime tradition. I am not concerned with propaganda films!

(He bangs the phone down and we see him turn to his fluttering secretary and say: "That man has gone insane! He wants to turn my museum into a sideshow!")

9

(As Terry fades out on the screen, the West Indian and the Nigerian approach Jackburn on stage.)

WEST INDIAN *(Gleefully):*
Man, you told him.

NIGERIAN:
I am sorry I spoke as I did. You are a real Captain.

JACKBURN:
Captain of nothing...Let's get the crew off the ship. Tell them we're making arrangements to send them home.

WEST INDIAN:
What are we going to do?

JACKBURN:
After they're off, I want to be left on board alone.

WEST INDIAN *(Indignantly, to Nigerian):*
Alone...You see what happens to your Nationalism?

NIGERIAN *(Snapping back):*
My nationalism is a great brotherhood of black men.

WEST INDIAN:
Man, your brothers are disappearing fast.

NIGERIAN *(To Jackburn):*
Why do you want to be alone on the ship?

JACKBURN:
It's better if you don't know.

196

WEST INDIAN *(Angrily)*:

There you are. Each black man to his own cell, his own country, his own clothes. *(With a gesture towards the Nigerian's clothes)*

NIGERIAN *(Angrily)*:

Do you want us to go around like apes in white clothes?

WEST INDIAN *(Scornfully)*:

I don't give a damn about clothes.

NIGERIAN *(Angrily)*:

My clothes are not nigger jeans and shirts, white man's servant clothes. With my clothes, I feel free. I can fly!

WEST INDIAN *(Scornfully)*:

Go on and fly! Nobody's criticizing your clothes. It's your brains, man.

JACKBURN *(With a smile)*:

Come on, I need your help. *(To the Nigerian)* I want you to go to the newspapers. Say that we're arranging the sale of the ship to Terry . . .

NIGERIAN:

But you told him off.

JACKBURN:

If they think we're negotiating, that will give me more time on the ship.

NIGERIAN:

Send someone else to the papers. I'll go with you.

WEST INDIAN *(Grinning)*:

Your brains are coming back, man. Count me in. At least we'll have a three-man nation on the ship.

JACKBURN *(With a smile of appreciation)*:

If that's the way you want it. I'll tell you my plan on the ship.

WEST INDIAN :

Here's to the three-man nation!

(They sing and mime part of "We're a Pretty Funny Nation" to end the scene.)

197

TRIO:

> Today, you've gotta be big.
> You've gotta have the highest brass,
> You can't sit on your ass.
> You've gotta have armies and navies,
> Officers and politicians,
> Factories and bureaucrats,
> Big lawyers,　　　and THINGS,
> If you want salvation as a nation...

(Then, slower, as they exit to the ship):

> But we're a pretty funny nation
> With a little boat for salvation...

10

(The flag is drawn up and the setting is back in the Tea Room. Miss Hooper and her brother are staring excitedly out the window at the ship. Peter and Laura are talking nervously. At stage right, Fanny and Johnny are still trying to persuade Carla.)

HOOPER:

They must have been persuaded to give up. They're getting ready to leave the ship.

MISS HOOPER:

I'm sorry in a way. It's been rather fun, I mean in the House of Commons...

HOOPER *(Annoyed)*:

Really, you romanticize everything. It's time these blacks were taken down a peg. You'll admit it's rather cheeky to enter the House...

MISS HOOPER *(Smiling)*:

Especially with you present, Michael.

HOOPER *(Snorting)*:

Nonsense! You're impossible.

MISS HOOPER *(Looking at Laura and Peter)*:

That American girl is taking it rather hard.

198

HOOPER:

Why shouldn't she? After all it's their Negro problem.

MISS HOOPER:

Is it? *(She sings the beginning of "The World Isn't White Any More.")*

> The world isn't white any more,
> The British lion doesn't whitely roar,

(Then, pointing at Laura and Peter)

> The American eagle doesn't whitely soar,
> The world isn't white any more ...

(The scene switches to Laura and Peter)

LAURA:

What'll happen to him?

PETER:

Who knows? You're not responsible.

LAURA:

He overheard me saying that he was mad. "That's a proposition to be considered," he said. "Maybe we're all mad ...." It's so easy to live in our old dream of a white world ... *(The four of them join in "The World Isn't White Any More.")*

> The world isn't white any more,

(With a gesture at the Hoopers)

> The British lion doesn't whitely roar,
> Our American eagle doesn't whitely soar,
> The world isn't white any more.

HOOPER *(Singing to his sister as they move closer to Peter and Laura):*

> How can the lion and the eagle mate?
> The British and the Yanks cooperate?
> Oh, we've got to have a new alliance
> In this ghastly age of science ...

MISS HOOPER:

> Since the world isn't white any more.

PETER *(Singing loudly in reply):*

> In Britain white was white and black
> Was blacker than a coal-black sack.
> In such a world of tea and power,
> The white man had his whitest hour . . .

LAURA:

> But the world isn't white any more.
> *(The four of them are now playing increasingly together.)*

MISS HOOPER:

> There was a time when our Na-vy
> Sailed whitely over the whitecapped sea
> And churchmen in their whitest faces
> Blessed the poor, un-Christian races,
> But the world isn't white any more.

LAURA:

> We think that we're a melting pot
> To cook a freedom that is hot,
> But then the pot we try to sell
> For profits that cook up a smell.
> The world isn't white any more.
> *(All move together gingerly, suspiciously, and sing.)*

ALL:

> The world isn't white any more,
> The British lion doesn't whitely roar,
> The American eagle doesn't whitely soar,
> The world isn't white any more.

MISS HOOPER:

> How can the lion and the eagle mate?

PETER:

> The British and the Yanks cooperate?

LAURA:

> Oh, we've got to have a new alliance . . .

HOOPER:

> In this ghastly age of science . . .

ALL:

> Since the world isn't white any more.
> The world isn't white any more,
> The British lion doesn't whitely roar,
> The American eagle doesn't whitely soar,
> The world isn't white any more.

(At the end of this ensemble song, they go to the window and continue to argue as they stare at the activity on the ship.)

11

FANNY *(To Carla)*:
Have you changed your mind, dearie?

JOHNNY:
You're the only one who can give an eyewitness story of the ship.

FANNY:
They'll pay plenty.

CARLA:
I told you I won't help you.

FANNY:
The press will be nasty if you don't cooperate. *(She improvises a mocking headline)* "White Girl Visits Ship With Pirate Captain!"

JOHNNY:
"Spanish Girl's Romance With Negro Navigator!"

FANNY:
"Black Captain Invites Spanish Girl Aboard To Love Nest!"

CARLA:
It wasn't like that!

FANNY *(Mockingly)*:
Who'll know the difference?

JOHNNY:
You'll get more red-hot publicity than Cleopatra.

CARLA *(Pleading, to Johnny)*:
Please, Johnny, you must understand. You're young...

201

(She sings, "When You Are Young.")

> When you are young
>> No river runs silently into the sea,
>> No ship sails quietly into the night.
> When you are young
>> Every voyage is a dream of freedom,
>> A salute of love, a flag of light.
>
> When you are young
>> Each ship is the horizon of your hope
>> And if it sinks there, every lover's voice
> (When you are young)
>> Will sing it back into its voyage,
>> For only love can make the air rejoice.

(A pause after the song, which has affected Johnny. Then Fanny begins to taunt Carla.)

FANNY:

It's a black ship sailing in your crazy dream. They'll send you back to Spain faster'n you can wink!

JOHNNY *(Abruptly):*

Let her alone...

FANNY *(Surprised):*

Don't forget we need Her Hoyal Highness...

JOHNNY:

We can handle it ourselves.

FANNY:

We don't know nothing about what happened on the ship.

JOHNNY:

So what? She doesn't know any better. She's young...

FANNY *(Angrily):*

So I'm an *old* biddy?

JOHNNY:

Let it go!

FANNY *(Disgusted):*

Well, I'll be...

12

(Hooper turns away from the window, as the Naval Officer enters with several men.)

HOOPER:

They're coming off the ship!

PETER:

Look at Jackburn!

MISS HOOPER *(Laughing):*

He's gorgeous!

LAURA:

What's that around his waist?

MISS HOOPER:

It's a sword!

NAVAL OFFICER *(Ill at ease):*

Stand back, please.

MISS HOOPER:

He's all dressed up for a ceremony!

NAVAL OFFICER *(Uncomfortably):*

That's his idea.

HOOPER *(Burning):*

You mean Her Majesty's Government is forced to undergo a Ceremony of Surrender?

NAVAL OFFICER *(Indignantly):*

They are surrendering, Sir.

HOOPER *(Hissing):*

Compromise, that's what it is, Sir, compromise.

(The crew members have been filing in. Jackburn appears in a superbly colorful, absurd, full-dress uniform, with a bright sword gleaming around his waist.)

JACKBURN:

Commander, are you ready to receive the official surrender of *The Black President?*

NAVAL OFFICER *(Stiffly):*
We're ready.

HOOPER *(Hissing):*
It's appeasement, Sir.

JACKBURN:
Advance and be recognized.

NAVAL OFFICER *(Angrily, trying to restrain himself):*
I believe *you* are the surrendering officer.

JACKBURN *(Genially):*
So I am. I'll come down then.

NAVAL OFFICER:
Is every man off the ship?

JACKBURN:
/Two are left. They'll be here shortly. Meanwhile, I'll turn over my sword.

NAVAL OFFICER *(Stiffly):*
Thank you, that won't be necessary.

JACKBURN:
I insist on the proper procedure.

NAVAL OFFICER *(Protesting):*
We don't carry swords in the modern navy except on dress occasions.

JACKBURN:
But this is a dress occasion... *(He pulls the sword out of its sheath)* *Sword*—"a hand weapon, with a longish blade, and thus distinct from all missile weapons on the one hand, and on the other hand from staff weapons such as the pike, bill, halberd and the like..." Source of information, *The Encyclopedia.* (He laughs) Really a peace weapon nowadays... *(The Naval Officer advances to take the sword. Suddenly, Jackburn points it at him as if in a duel.)* En garde! We are not quite ready to surrender... In history we are told that uncivilized people use only the edge of the sword... *(He demonstrates and the Naval Officer shrinks back.)* The mark of a superior civilization is the knowledge of how to use the point. *(He demonstrates again to the Naval Officer's distress.)* In the

Renaissance, of course, the sword became a true, thrusting weapon, narrowed, finely pointed, influenced perhaps by the medieval German *panzerstecher,* that thrusting weapon carried by horsemen ... *(He demonstrates. Then he takes another sword from a crewman and tosses it to the Naval Officer. They stand facing each other for a duel. The Naval Officer is dazed by this development. Jackburn advances on the Naval Officer, who puts up his sword automatically to defend himself.)* When excited, the natural tendency is to cut with the sword. That's wrong, Commander. The thrust is the true maneuver ... *(He thrusts and the Naval Officer thrusts back.)* Good! Today we're back thrusting with swords, the sword and the rocket as true missile weapons! *(He thrusts and sweeps the sword out of the Naval Officer's hands. After a moment, mockingly, he holds his own sword up in both hands.)* I surrender ... He sings with the crew, "The Surrender of the Sword." The music is the same as in Scene 9, Part 1.)

JACKBURN:

> Across the sea we sail
> Until the world of white
> Sees through its twisted glass
> The black world of night.

THE CREW:

> Come on old Dame Freedom!
> Put on your mask of white.
> Lower *The Black President's* flag ...

(The flag is lowered as they sing. The music is slower, more satirical, not as jubilant as in Part 1. When the flag is almost down, the West Indian and the Nigerian rush in and signal to Jackburn.)

JACKBURN *(Shouting exultantly):*
Ready! Fire!

(An explosion is heard from the river. People at the window cry out, "The ship! They've blown up the ship! etc.")

JACKBURN *(Handing his sword to the dazed Naval Officer):*
We dedicate this sunken ship as an international underwater monument to the voyage of *The Black President!*

205

THE CREW *(Jubilantly now)*:

> Come on, old Dame Freedom!
> Tear off your mask of white.
> Raise The Black President's flag!

(The flag shoots up again.)

13

(A film sequence. The television commentator of Part 1 appears.)

COMMENTATOR:

We bring you a final report on the strange adventure of *The Black President,* which ended dramatically yesterday when Captain Moses Jackburn blew up his ship in the Thames. Our first guest is Sir Reginald Denhurst, Lord of the Admiralty. Sir Reginald, why did Jackburn blow up his ship?

SIR REGINALD *(Guarded tone)*:

Well, we have his statement, although we can't be certain of his motives. It seems that he was afraid of having his ship confiscated on the high seas. Perhaps he realized the absurdity of his voyage ...

COMMENTATOR:

Absurdity?

SIR REGINALD:

Impossibility if you wish to call it that. These things are better handled by the proper legal channels.

COMMENTATOR:

What will happen to him and his crew?

SIR REGINALD:

They'll be deported, I assume, for illegal entry.

COMMENTATOR:

Will other charges be preferred against them?

SIR REGINALD:

As far as I know, no further charges will be pressed. Fortunately, despite the impulsive nature of Jackburn's act, no one was injured.

COMMENTATOR:

Sir Reginald, you stated previously that one of Jackburn's motives was an effort to abolish Nationalism. Do you have a final comment on this?

SIR REGINALD *(Guardedly):*

Well, as I said before, Nationalism is Nationalism. You can't just abolish it. While the world must move closer together for the maintenance of peace, it seems clear that a man is born in his own country and must follow his own customs ...

(As we see by the expression on the commentator's face, this is exactly what Sir Reginald said before.)

COMMENTATOR:

Yes, well, thank you, Sir Reginald ... We go now to Lagos, Nigeria, for further comment by Nkrume Okolo, the head of the Nigerian Freedom Party, and Michael Daviers, the Chairman of the African Unilateralist Committee. Mr. Okolo, what do you think of the end of Captain Jackburn's voyage?

OKOLO:

The defiant gesture of Captain Jackburn in sinking his ship demonstrates that he has discovered the necessity of black unity. I regret only that he was not able to sail to South Africa! *(He sings a refrain from "Black Africa.")*

> Black Africa is what we need to build,
> Black Africa first!

COMMENTATOR:

Thank you, Mr. Okolo. Mr. Daviers, what is your opinion of the end of Captain Jackburn's voyage?

DAVIERS:

It seems clear that Captain Jackburn sank his ship in the cause of world peace. This is what he meant by "international underwater monument." He wanted to demonstrate the absurdity of war in a world haunted by nuclear weapons.

(He sings a refrain from "Why Can't a Unilateralist Be Black?")

> Why can't a unilateralist be black? ...

OKOLO *(Interrupting to begin the argument again):*

That's all very well, Daviers, but you can't stop the independence struggle with your fantastic world dream...

DAVIERS:

I am *not* against independence! What about the bomb? Is that black or white?

(They sing a brief, fierce duet again.)

OKOLO:

> Black Africa is what we need to build,
> > Black Africa first!
> Black nation after nation with their power
> > To cool black thirst,
> > Black Africa first!

DAVIERS:

> Why can't a unilateralist be black?
> The atom bomb is not a stone
> And will not fall on white alone.
> Why can't a unilateralist be black?...

(Again we realize by the commentator's expression that this is a repetition of their former argument.)

COMMENTATOR:

Thank you, Mr. Okolo and Mr. Daviers. We had hoped to bring you some official comment on Jackburn's voyage from the American government, but American officials have refused any comment. They state that it was a private voyage and, consequently, has absolutely nothing to do with American foreign policy. However, we have for you a final interview with Captain Jackburn's countryman, the oil magnate, Mr. Frank Terry. Mr. Terry, is it true that Jackburn called you just before he sank the ship?

TERRY:

Yes, he wanted to sell me his ship, but his terms were absurd. I was to turn the ship into a degrading exhibition of slavery by hiring unemployed colored men to demonstrate the actual conditions of slave-ship life.

COMMENTATOR *(Gaping):*
Unemployed colored men?...

TERRY:

That's right. He sounded out of his mind. He called them nig . . .

(He stops, not wanting to say the word on TV, and the commentator comes in quickly.)

COMMENTATOR:

One minor point . . . Why did Jackburn call his ship *The Black President?*

TERRY *(Shrugging)*:

I have no idea. Perhaps he wishes to stress his pride in the fact that there are now many colored presidents of African nations. However, I would like to praise the British government for the generous and discreet way in which they handled this little adventure. I am sure that the British-American alliance will continue to foster the great principles of peace and freedom for which they have always struggled.

(Again the commentator's face reveals his awareness of the repetition of Terry's words.)

COMMENTATOR:

Thank you, Mr. Terry. We would have liked to end our program with an interview with Captain Jackburn. But, as he is being held for deportation, that is impossible at the moment. Next, the weather report . . .

(The program ends with the beginning of a typical British weather report.)

14

(In front of the flag, a few pieces of nondescript furniture indicate the room where Jackburn is being held until he is deported. The Naval Officer enters.)

NAVAL OFFICER:

There's a girl to see you.

JACKBURN:

I thought visitors were banned.

NAVAL OFFICER:

You're sailing tonight.

JACKBURN:

Home sweet home . . . You don't waste any time.

NAVAL OFFICER:

Some of your crew have sailed already. The Americans will be on
your ship.

JACKBURN *(Ironically)*:

Hail Nationalism, blacks to the black countries, whites to the white
countries, and Americans to the old black and white checkerboard
game.

NAVAL OFFICER *(Stiffly)*:

I am merely doing my duty in an unusual case.

JACKBURN *(Smiling)*:

Same here. I'm just trying to darken the world a bit.

NAVAL OFFICER:

Shall I let her in? It's the Spanish girl. She says that she is pregnant
. . . *(Jackburn stares at him and begins to laugh.)* I don't see that
it's so funny.

JACKBURN:

Of course it's funny. I've been going around London in my free time
impregnating white women. That's all the black man wants to do.
It's part of our plan to turn the world black. We're the big, black,
sexual nightmare.

NAVAL OFFICER:

I assure you I am not interested in your nightmares. She's being sent
back to Spain, but she wants to see you before she sails.

(Jackburn shrugs. The Naval Officer goes out, and Carla enters.)

JACKBURN *(Bitterly)*:

When is the baby due?

CARLA:

It was the only way I could see you.

JACKBURN:

How much did the newspapers pay?

CARLA :

Nothing. Please believe me.

JACKBURN :

You won't be too welcome in Spain.

CARLA :

I could not go without seeing you when I do not know the end.

JACKBURN :

You think I know that?

CARLA :

I think you have an idea what you do.

JACKBURN :

You're a funny girl. We're sailing in opposite directions. Look up a white man in Spain.

CARLA :

In Spain we favor black colors. The old women wear black forever in mourning. We write our letters with big, black lines around them to respect the dead. Even our religion is black. You see often a black Christ on a black cross.

JACKBURN :

Don't hang me up on that cross, girl. I don't like that kind of black when Christ and torture get mixed up.

CARLA :

When I was young, the priest always told me about a dark god of suffering. I search for him, but I never find . . .

JACKBURN :

Don't give me this crap about a dark god. When I was a kid, writhing on the floor of the church, shouting out "Hallelujah!", staring up in the air at God, I saw his color was *white*. He'd put his big, white hand down, and the longest, white fingers you ever saw in your life touched me on the shoulder. And I cried out in fear, "God, you're white!" And he said, "Of course. You're my black son." And I screamed back, "If I'm your black son, how come I can't go piss in the white man's toilet in the railroad station?" Those long, white fingers dug into my shoulder again, and that deep, white voice said,

"Black son, when you get to heaven, there aren't going to be any black and white toilets. Up here you're going to have a blazing white skin at last." I wanted that white skin more than anything else . . . But one day I heard that deep, white voice say, "The black man wants to rape your white sisters! The black man wants to pour his dark seed through the world!" Suddenly, the only thing I wanted to do was look in a mirror and say, "Look, a black man." That's all, just those simple words, "Look, a black man."

CARLA *(Softly, looking at him):*
Look, a black man . . .

JACKBURN *(Savagely):*
Go away, white girl, go back to your dark country. Walk into your old, cold churches and kneel before your black Christ. He's not really black. That sun's burned him dark, that's all. He's got the longest white fingers in the world. He can grab anything he wants.

CARLA:
You are so bitter. I liked you better when you were on your ship. Then you were gay. The darkness began to sing.

JACKBURN:
The darkness has stopped singing. The age of romance is over. Nobody laughed much at my big joke.

CARLA:
I laughed. I think maybe young people all over the world laugh. When I go back to Spain, I want to keep laughing, even if I'm alone.

JACKBURN:
Go ahead and laugh. Who's stopping you?

CARLA:
Why did you really sink the ship? For yourself?

JACKBURN:
I don't know . . . For myself mainly. End of the line, end of the joke . . .

CARLA:
Why did you call your ship, *The Black President?*

JACKBURN:

Why should I tell you? So we can kiss and part and be Romeo and Juliet forever after?

CARLA:

I don't think you're Romeo. I think you're a man turned bitter, and I have never dreamed much of being Juliet. When you took me to see your ship, I thought this is crazy. These black people are all wearing masks. That's the only way they can sing and dance and laugh. That's the only way they can build a ship called *The Black President*. It's a crazy name. What does it mean? . . . I'm not sure I want to know . . . *(She turns away):*

JACKBURN:

All right I'll tell you. So you can go home and sleep in peace . . . . The last Port of Honor was going to be Washington, D. C. We were going to launch that ship on the Potomac and stop, bang, at the capitol. Then we were going to hold a big meeting right there in front of all that history of white democracy. And right there I was going to announce the biggest joke of all . . . *(A pause.)*

CARLA:

The biggest joke?

JACKBURN:

My campaign as The Black President. The first real campaign of a black man for President of the United States.

CARLA:

You are bitter.

JACKBURN:

Not in the beginning. Then I wanted it to be a funny joke—so funny you could hear the black laughter over the boiling black skins. I'd stand in front of the Capitol, maybe only a small audience at first, and I'd say . . .

(The screen lights up to show Jackburn in front of the Capitol in Washington addressing a small group of people. His image on the screen gestures and orates, while he speaks from the stage.)

Ladies and gentlemen, we've had every kind of religion for President except Jewish. Now we're going to start in on the color of

213

skin. We're going to have a black skin first, and maybe a yellow skin later. Consider the effect of a Black President in the White House. You want a scrapegoat, don't make him unemployed, make him President! Segregate him in the White House! *(Silent laughter among the audience on the screen)* I promise to look at everything through black color. We'll have some perspective again. Throw a pigeon in the air hundreds of miles away and he heads straight for home. That's the kind of direction we want. Vote for Jackburn, your black, homing pigeon! My program is simple. I've got three points: Peace Weapons, Sex, and Religion!

CARLA *(Laughing)*:
Peace Weapons, Sex and Religion?

JACKBURN *(Laughing with her)*:
That's it, lady. Laugh! Come on, Mr. President. Take your campaign to the country. New York!

(The screen shows Jackburn being greeted in New York. The crew is heard singing.)

CHORUS:

> Three points for President!
> Peace Weapons, Sex, and Religion!
> Vote for Jackburn,
> Your black homing pigeon!

JACKBURN *(His figure on the screen is seen exhorting the audience, as he speaks from the stage)*:
Take my first point, Peace Weapons. Not too many black physicists worked on the H-Bomb. The whole trouble is all of our new weapons were named by whites. That H-Bomb has got too much of the feeling of Old Nick and the burning fires behind it. And those missiles with names like Nike and Titan and Jupiter. Everything is ass-backward, folks. Who ever heard of a rocket named The Winged Goddess of Victory? That's what we'll have next. We've got too many classicists naming our weapons. You ever heard of a rocket named Jesus Christ? Or an intercontinental missile named Schweitzer or Einstein? What we've got to do is change all the names of weapons into peace names. Nobody's going

214

to drop an H-Bomb named Saint Francis, Saint Augustine, or even Saint Paul! Look at everything from a fresh, black point of view. We'll name all those missiles for peace instead of war. We'll build up a new army of Peace Weapons!

(Silent laughter on the screen. The chorus is heard singing.)

CHORUS:

> Three points for President!
> Peace Weapons, Sex, and Religion!
> Vote for Jackburn,
> Your black homing pigeon!

JACKBURN:

On to Chicago! Take the Midwest by storm!
   (The screen shows Jackburn in Chicago. A bigger crowd is evident. The camera focuses on several faces in the crowd laughing with delight.)

I'm very happy to present the second point in my platform to you people of Chicago. *Sex.* You ever heard that mentioned honestly in a political campaign? In the past, presidential candidates have just kissed babies and old ladies. But what does your Black President say about sex? Does he say rape all the white ladies? My platform is very simple .... I want all of you white people — Republicans, Democrats, Prohibitionists, everybody — to get together and nominate your ideal white woman for Vice-President. Then, I promise you, as Black President, I'll marry your white Vice President. I'll take on that chore and we'll have a true public forum for all the problems of integration. I'll take on your white burdens! We'll have a TV show every Sunday, a Press Conference every Monday: Mr. and Mrs. Black and White!

CARLA *(Laughing)*:
   I'll run for Vice-President!

JACKBURN:
   You can't. You're Spanish.

CARLA:
   I'll immigrate!

JACKBURN:

The Statue of Liberty, 150 feet high, welcomes you. The Black President announces his integrated campaign with the white Vice-President . . . Hail, Mr. and Mrs. Black and White!

(On the screen, we see Jackburn and Carla together, hailed by a large crowd. Shots of Carla and Jackburn are interspersed with shots of people in the crowd laughing.)

CHORUS *(Singing)*:

Hail, Mr. and Mrs. Black and White!
Let the standards of integration
Be set at the highest station.
Hail, Mr. and Mrs. Black and White,
You're a liberating sight!

(The screen shows Carla about to address a large crowd.)

CARLA:

People of America I greet you. Your Statue of Liberty, 150 feet high, has gathered me in with its welcoming arms. I am a Spanish girl. I am full of prejudice. I have read about your country only in newspapers and film star magazines. I am a white girl brought up by a white God. Therefore, I am eligible to run as your white Vice-President. The first black man I saw was in a film. The second black man I saw was a servant. The third black man I saw I fell in love with, and so I'll sing you my acceptance. *(She sings.)*

As Mrs. Black and White
I'll serve you day and night;
A white Vice-President
From Spain I have been sent

To integrate for your delight.
We'll live a public life
When I become his wife
And serve as Mrs. Black and White.

(The screen shows them together in various intimate, homemaking shots, interspersed with shots of the public laughing and applauding.)

216

CARLA and JACKBURN *(Singing together)*:

> We're Mr. and Mrs. Black and White,
> We integrate for your delight.
> Our public marriage is a cure
> For your desire to be pure.
>
> The burdens of your racial hate
> We take as our true marriage fate,
> As Mr. and Mrs. Black and White
> To integrate by day and night.

(The screen shows quick public and private shots of Mr. and Mrs. Black and White's campaign across the country. Many laughing faces are seen in the crowds and among the people meeting Mr. and Mrs. Black and White.)

JACKBURN *(Speaking)*:

San Francisco! End of the line. The black homing pigeon comes to the end of the frontier to present the final point in my campaign — Religion!

(Shots of Mr. and Mrs. Black and White crossing the Golden Gate Bridge, driving past the City Hall, etc. The Chorus is heard singing.)

CHORUS:

> Three points for President!
> Peace Weapons, Sex, and Religion!
> Vote for Jackburn,
> Your black homing pigeon!

(Shots of Jackburn and Carla waving to crowd. Jackburn steps forward to speak.)

JACKBURN:

Here in San Francisco, the frontier ends in the Pacific Ocean. Something new has to begin, and that's religion. We've had those Greek gods led by Zeus with his blasting thunderbolt...

(A shot of a heroic, wrathful statue of Zeus hurling a thunderbolt at man is shown on the screen.)

217

We've had the crucified Jesus . . .

(A shot of Christ on the cross — from a famous traditional painting — is shown on the screen.)

We've had the beautiful, meditative Buddha . . .

(A shot of one of the impressive statues of the contemplative Buddha is shown on the screen.)

We've had the great Arabian prophet, Mohammed . . .

(A shot of Mohammed is shown on the screen.)

But none of them has brought peace to the black and white men. So it's clear we need a new religion in America. We need a God who's not just a God of agony and suffering and who doesn't always have a white skin. Let him be a Laughing God of Many Colors, half of his face black, half white . . .

(Shots of a powerful, laughing God with half of his face black and the other half white.)

Let the hands with which he serves the world be red . . .

(Shots of huge red hands.)

And the legs on which he strides through the world be yellow . . .

(Shot of long, yellow legs striding through vast, open country.)

Above all, let him laugh! Whenever your nerves begin to twitch with resentment or the boredom of your life; whenever you're about to explode, listen to the Laughing God.

(A shot of the Laughing God.)

But I warn you . . . He won't laugh away your sins. He hasn't got a big, white handkerchief to wipe up your tears. All he does is laugh and you've got to make something from his laughter. Sometimes you'll think it's a crazy laugh of a god who doesn't know what to do about all the different races, a god who's gone mad trying to blend all those colors together. Other times you'll think he's laughing just because he wants to laugh. All you've got to do is make what you need out of his laughter. You've got to find something in your hatred and love and desire to make you human again and not just a walking mirror reflecting the old black or white straitjackets. So vote for Mr. and Mrs. Black and White and the Laughing God of Many Colors!

(Shots of the Laughing God behind Jackburn and Carla, interspersed with shots of laughing faces in the crowd. The Chorus, Carla, and Jackburn sing.)

CHORUS:

> Hail, Mr. and Mrs. Black and White.
> Let the standards of integration
> Be set at the highest station.
> Hail, Mr. and Mrs. Black and White,
> You're a liberating sight!

CARLA and JACKBURN:

> Hail to the Laughing God
> Of Many Colors!
> His yellow legs go
> Striding through the world;
> His red hands reach out
> To touch all men;
> His black and white face
> Laughs to bring us grace.

CHORUS:

> Hail, Mr. and Mrs. Black and White!
> Hail to the Laughing God
> Of Many Colors!

(Suddenly, the screen goes dark. There is a knock on the door and the Naval Officer enters.)

NAVAL OFFICER:
It's time to go.

JACKBURN *(Crying out to Carla):*
What'll you do back in Spain?

CARLA:
I don't know ... *(She sings.)*

Spain is a memory of freedom
That I'm too young to know,
A beginning that went bad,
A spring that turned to snow . . .

JACKBURN *(Singing):*
A beginning that went bad,
A harvest never sown . . .

TOGETHER:

What can you do if a beginning is bad?
You work for an ending that's good.

CARLA *(To Jackburn, as the Naval Officer escorts her out):*
Goodbye . . . Good luck on your campaign. *(They exit.)*

JACKBURN *(Abruptly, shouting through the door after them):*
God damn the campaign! You hear me? It's all a pile of shit! You
can't laugh off a black skin. You can't laugh the world into peace.
They'll train you, they'll beat you, buy you into order. When I get
back to New York, I'm going off and hide in the loneliest, black
room in the city. I'm going to be the original, invisible man! All
of you bastards who are trying to fix up the world can go stuff
yourselves! You hear me? *(He leans against the door, crying.)*

15

*(The screen lights up to show the slave ship, "The Black President,"
sailing across the ocean. The Chorus of the crew is heard singing.)*

CHORUS:

Where's that ship gonna sail?
Sail here, sail there, sail everywhere.
Jackburn sail, Jackburn free . . .

*(Slowly, Jackburn moves away from the door to look up at the
screen and the image of his dream. He is trying to throw off the
bitterness of his last outburst, wondering what he will do. He
begins to sing.)*

220

JACKBURN:

> ...That grave is a little too welcome,
> Too cold under earth's floor,
> The bones don't sing any more...

(The Chorus comes in with "Sail, man, sail, sail everywhere," etc.)

> Maybe somewhere there's a little light,
> Not a big glare, not a sun
> In the sky as hot as a bomb,
> But enough to see by,
> A new world to be won...

CHORUS:

> Where's that ship gonna sail?
> Sail here, sail there, sail everywhere,
> Jackburn sail, Jackburn free,
> Jackburn got that freedom ship.
> Sail man, sail, sail everywhere!

(The lights fade slowly as Jackburn is staring at the ship sailing across the ocean.)

THE END